My Impressions
of America

Margot Asquith

MARGOT ASQUITH
  Returning from her visit to the White House.

MY IMPRESSIONS
OF AMERICA

BY

MARGOT ASQUITH

AUTHOR OF "MARGOT ASQUITH: AN AUTOBIOGRAPHY,"
ETC.

1922

CONTENTS

I.
ABOARD THE *CARMANIA*

MARGOT NOT A NATURAL TOURIST; LACKS CURIOSITY—
HEADLINES IN LONDON COMPARED WITH HEADLINES IN
NEW YORK—AMERICAN WOMEN WORLDLY—AMERICAN
MEN THE GENUINE ARTICLE

I MOTORED to Southampton on Saturday, the 21st of January, this year, and after saying good-bye to my husband and my son, retired to my berth on the *Carmania*. I am a bad traveller, and had been laid up with a sort of influenza until the day before I left London.

Kindly press people tempted me to confide in them on the ship. They asked me if I would be back in time for Princess Mary's wedding; where I was going when I arrived in America, and if I looked forward to my trip. I sometimes wonder what questions I would put if I were obliged to interview a traveller. I would ask with reluctance where they were going, but never what they had seen, because I know I could not listen to their answers. Everyone knows what you are likely to see if you go for any length of time to London, Rome, Athens or the United States; and is there a person living whose impressions you would care to hear either upon the Coliseum, Niagara Falls, or any other of the great works of art or of nature? On such subjects the remarks of the cleverest and stupidest are equally inadequate and the superb vocabulary of a Ruskin will probably not be more illuminating than what the school-boy writes in the Visitors' Book at Niagara, "Uncle and all very much pleased."

I am inclined to think it is a mild form of vanity that makes a certain type of rich person travel every year. I have heard these say that for all the interest we who are left behind take in what they have seen and heard, they might as well have remained at Brighton. Nevertheless, the world is full of tourists; and there are a number of people who like to pick up pieces of unimportant information without effort. The foolish majority of these read the *Daily Mail*; the political, the *Manchester Guardian*; the Liberals, the *Westminster Gazette*; the intellectual, the *New Statesman*; and to pass the time on Sundays there are always the long columns of the *Observer* or for the credulous, the "Secret History of the Week."

After glancing at the leading articles, the City man turns to "Round the Markets: Home Railways firm. The Chilian Scrip reacted to 1¼ premium and Norway sixes give way to ninety-five." They then read: "By the Silver Sea, the Sunny South, or Glowing East"; ponder over lists of those who are going to Egypt, America, or the Riviera; and end by learning that the site of the old General Post Office was in St. Martins-le-Grand.

In America it is rather different. On the front page of one of the most important papers you read:

"Kardos has hopes of father's aid," "Men faint in public and lose $153,000," "Death note writer caught in Capital," "Losses of women duped by Lindsay," "Iceland cabinet falls," "Tokio diet in uproar over snake on floor," "Saddle horse from Firestone, Harding's favourite mount," and short notices on Ireland, Paris and London; you are encouraged to turn to page 6, column five or column 8, page 5 and finish with "Dazzling display of Princess Mary's lingerie."

It is difficult to say why most travellers are uninteresting. I do not think it is because they have been to wonderful places, but because the average man has not the power to assimilate or interpret what he has seen; and they enlarge on their own sensations with such a lack of humour and proportion, that you feel as if they were not only rebuffing you, but claiming part of the credit of the master works themselves. When told at a party that you ought to meet Mr. So-and-So, as he has just come back from the Far East, Southwest, or North Pole, you cling to the nearest door post, and make your escape while the hero is being traced in the crowd. I like what I have thought out for myself better than what I discover; and conclusions arrived at after careful reflection are more enlarging than what is pointed out to you by inquisitive spectators.

I am not a natural tourist, and Napoleon's shaving soap will never interest me as much as the smallest light upon his mind or character. There is a difference between curiosity and interest, and I regret to say I am not curious.

I have come to the United States for the first time, not in a missionary spirit or to study anything or anybody, but to see my daughter and to enjoy myself.

In a rash moment, however, I promised to write my impressions of the United States and Canada, and this may give rise to false hopes.

Lord Acton wrote in a letter to Mrs. Drew, "One touch of ill nature makes the whole world kin," and I must make an effort not to disappoint my thoughtful critics. I have been accused of failing to appreciate the society of brilliant American women whether in Italy,

Paris or London; but it could be added with truth that brilliance, while stimulating most people, has always exhausted me. I prefer the clumsiest thought to the most finished phrase, and am so slow, that the mildest complication may make me miss the point. "General and prolonged laughter" is a faculty I have never been able to acquire, and sudden explosions over anything I have said usually convince me that I had better have held my tongue.

To an outsider who has only known European Americans, the most noticeable thing about American women is their freedom from native soil. They are equally well equipped whether their nationality is transferred from Russia to Rome, Vienna, Roumania or Paris. No blank cheque could be more adequately filled in, and I never cease wondering what can be the secret of their perfect social mechanism.

Beautiful to look at and elegantly dressed, with an open mind upon whatever topic is discussed, adaptable, available, rich and good-humoured, the American woman as I know her is the last word in worldiness and fashion. In my own country she is not only a popular, but a privileged person, and having started by being what is called "natural," she becomes more and more so every day.

The husbands of these ladies, when not of needy foreign aristocracy, are usually divorced, discharged or disposed of in some way or other; and, even if they are of the same nationality, are quite unlike the American man as I have known him.

He is seldom fashionable and never leisured; he has a passion for learning all that there is to be known, and holds vigorous views upon most things. If a little copious in narrative, he is never mechanical, but an absolutely genuine article; spontaneous, friendly, hospitable and keen. He appears to treat his women folk with the patience and indulgence you extend to spoilt children, never attempting to discuss matters, either literary or political, with them, and is agreeably surprised if you show an interest in Wall Street or the White House.

I am jotting down these preliminary impressions, any one of which may—and probably will—have to be revised during the course of my travels.

II.
ARRIVAL IN NEW YORK

REPORTERS LACKING IN AWE—SPLENDOURS OF HOTEL
LIFE—FIRST LECTURE A FAILURE AS RESULT OF SEA-
SICKNESS—THRILLED BY NEW YORK'S ARCHITECTURE

AFTER an abominable voyage during which the ship rolled and
rocked, groaned and shuddered, and the sea did precisely what it
liked with us, we arrived a day and a half late, and surrounded by
press-men I feather-stitched on to American soil.

If the reporters are a little lacking in awe, they make up for it by the
intelligent interest they take in everything connected with one; and
after being asked what I thought of "flappers" and what Mr. Lloyd
George thought of me, I was allowed to go to the Ambassador Hotel.
I could not have been greeted with more courtesy had I arrived at
Windsor Castle, nor have I ever stayed in a better hotel.

My son-in-law Prince Bibesco, my daughter Elizabeth, and my
cousin Miss Tennant (whose brother is Sir Auckland Geddes's
private secretary), showed me the airy bedrooms and beautiful
bathrooms which the manager of the hotel had chosen for us. I sat
down completely exhausted when suddenly the door opened and
my sitting room was flooded with male and female reporters.
Having been seasick and without solid food for a week, the carpet
and ceiling were still nodding at me, and I regret to confess that I
said nothing very striking; but they were welcoming and friendly;
and after a somewhat dislocated conversation I staggered off to bed.

I was introduced the next day by my cicerone, Mr. Lee Keedick, to
the New Amsterdam Theatre, where scouts were placed in distant
galleries to try my voice. I had no difficulty in making myself heard,
but I felt terribly ill and more than inadequate as I made my first
appearance at 3.30 in the well filled theatre. Dr. Murray Butler
introduced me in a courteous speech and explained that after such
an unusually rough crossing I would be obliged to sit down
throughout the performance, which I much regretted.

I opened with a spirited account of an Irish horse dealer, which, I
could see at a glance, interested nobody. Whether I was speaking
Irish or English, it might have been Walloon for all the audience
cared. My heart faded, my voice sank, and I knew that many could
not hear; some were not listening, and my friends were watching me

with apprehension, charity and cheers. More dead than alive I was relieved when an enterprising lady shouted from the gallery:

"You've got my money for nothing—Good-bye, I've had enough of you!"

This informal greeting stirred the kindness of my listeners to a protest, and as soon as I could, I changed to other subjects. With the fall of the curtain many old friends came on to the stage, and presenting me with roses, assured me that I had won the hearts of my audience, after which I left the theatre.

Driving home, I opened all the taxi windows and was struck with the architectural beauties of the streets. With the exception of Munich I have never seen a modern town comparable to New York. The colour of the stone and lightness of the air would put vitality into a corpse; and in spite of a haunting recollection that the lady in the gallery had had enough of me, I returned to the Ambassador happy though exhausted.

My daughter took me in the evening to a wonderful party given by Miss Mabel Gerry. We wore our best clothes, but our taxi driver did not seem satisfied, and before turning in to the magnificent court-yard, he stopped, opened the door, and enquired rather sceptically if this was where we were expected; concealing our mortification we urged him to drive on.

There was something for every taste at Miss Gerry's beautiful house. I started by sitting next to my dear old friend Mr. Harry White, and a brilliant stranger Mr. Thomas Ridgeway; went on to play bridge, listened to a fluent pianist, and finished by dancing unknown steps to a wonderful band.

I am enunciating a platitude when I say the Americans are the finest dancers in the world.

III.
BOSTON AND WORCESTER

DISCOMFORT OF TRAVEL IN AMERICA—STAGE FRIGHT IN
BOSTON—BOSTONIANS INTELLIGENT AND COURTEOUS—
JOHN SARGENT'S FRESCOES IN THE MUSEUM

ON the 2nd of February, next morning, my friend and secretary Mr. Horton, myself and maid arrived in Boston City after a comfortable journey in a private compartment given to us by the courtesy of our guard. I do not wish to say anything disagreeable, but except for the beauty of the railway stations, the travelling arrangements in America are far inferior to ours. Sitting erect on revolving chairs in public, is a trial not lessened by an atmosphere in which you could force pineapples. We were greeted upon our arrival by reporters and cameras. It distresses me to stand blinking at the sun; as not being a beauty, I know that my nose will always be more of a limb than a feature, and trying to look pleasant results in my teeth coming out like tombstones in the morning papers.

Left to ourselves, we went to examine the Symphony Hall, where I was to speak that night. Arriving on the stage, I stood appalled. Feeling like a midge upon a dreadnought, I looked at the largest hall I have ever seen, except the one in London erected to the sacred memory of good Prince Albert.

"This is a practical joke of the worst kind!" I exclaimed to the gentlemen in attendance, "and not for a million dollars would I insult the Boston people by making myself ridiculous here to-night. I have not been in prison, or divorced; nor have I been to the North or South Pole, or climbed mountains and Matterhorns; I have nothing wonderful to tell about, and instead of one woman shouting, 'Give me back my money—I've had enough of you,' the whole audience will rise to their feet. This is not a hall, it's a railway tunnel! I cannot see the end of it: it's made for engines or aeroplanes"; and I trembled with rage and apprehension.

"It's a concert hall, madam, built for oratorios," they replied, pointing to a vast organ decorating the wall behind me.

"No doubt drums, trumpets, or opera singers could make themselves heard, but a shrimp of a female standing alone here would make the gods laugh, and nothing will induce me to speak!"

"But, dear madam, all Boston is coming to hear you."

Mr. Horton put his arm through mine, saying soothingly, "You are tired; let us go back to the hotel."

Visibly distressed, the gentlemen of the hall assured me that men of meagre voice had lectured many times and been perfectly heard; and as I walked away I saw through the corner of my eyes that my angelic secretary was nodding to assure them that I would keep my contract.

Alone in the taxi I burst into tears, asking what I had done to be so punished; I said that the front rows would be deafened, the centre bewildered, and the balconies indignant. He assured me I had a beautiful voice, an interesting personality and a plucky nature, etc., and that I must certainly go through with it as every seat had been sold.

I dressed with streaming eyes and a scarlet nose, and in snow and silence we drove to the Symphony Hall. The platform and auditorium were crowded, and blind with fear, I walked on to the front of the stage. My chairman, Mr. Arthur Hill (Corporation Counsel of the City of Boston), in introducing me spoke with the greatest ease, and I observed that every word he said was heard; but it was obvious from the perfection of his speech that he had addressed a thousand audiences before and this was only my second public appearance.

I stood up with my knees knocking together as I looked at the sea of expectant faces below me.

Heaven forefend that I should repeat what I said, but for one hour and twenty minutes I did the best I could; beginning with my pleasure at being in America, I continued with stories of my native land, and ended with an account of Windsor Castle and the Disarmament Conference.

No president or prime minister could have had a more intelligent, friendly, courteous and responsive audience than the people of Boston. Aching from my ankles to my temples, I bowed to their repeated cheers as, humble and happy, I retired from the stage.

Enthusiastic hearers pressed into the green room where I had sunk into a chair as immovable as the mangle. Mr. Horton, who had sat among the statues on the sky line, assured me he had heard every syllable. Eager reporters began to ask what I thought of Boston, but dumb and exhausted I bundled into my cloak. Crowds of men and women were waiting in the street, and as I motored away I gathered I had been a success.

The next day Lieutenant Governor Alvin Fuller and his wife—who were among those who had congratulated me in the green room the night before—gave us lunch and took us in their motor to the two great Boston sights: the Public Library and the Fine Arts Museum.

The Library is a magnificent building, founded in 1852, containing over two million volumes, half of which are lent out for daily use at home. The architects of the building were McKim, Mead, & White of New York, but most of the design was the work of Charles Follen McKim. The mural decorations were painted by Puvis de Chavannes, Edwin Austin Abbey, and John Singer Sargent. As my time was limited I concentrated on the works of my friend Mr. Sargent.

It would be as impossible as it would be pretentious to attempt to describe the beauty of the Sargent Hall. It represents thirty years of thought and labour, and has a majesty of design, glory of drawing, and originality of conception unequalled by anything in Europe.

The "Hand-Maid of the Lord" on the east wall, holding the Divine Child in her arms, and "Our Lady of Sorrows," which faces it, fill your heart with wonder and your eyes with tears.

In the first, the Blessed Virgin is rising from a throne with her baby in her arms. You realise in looking at this Child that He is the Mighty God and Everlasting Father; and the expression on the face of the Virgin—more than of any other Madonna that I have ever seen—convinces you that she was not only the Mother of the Counsellor upon whose shoulders the Government would fall, but the Mother of the Prince of Peace.

The Virgin in "Our Lady of Sorrows" stands upon the crescent moon behind a row of lighted candles raised in relief of white, gold and silver. Her little face with wide-set eyes looks down upon you from an elaborate silver crown set against a radiant halo of fine and illusive design, and her two beautiful hands clasp to her heart the shining swords that typify the Seven Sorrows. The dignity of her pose, the submission and pathos of her haunting eyes waken you to a new sense of the majesty of pain. I felt, as I looked up, that I was sharing a common gratitude that such subjects should have captured the genius of the greatest living artist.

We went on from the Library to the Museum, where the decorations of the dome of the rotunda, to say nothing of the exterior of the buildings, are magnificent. Here Mr. John Sargent has surpassed himself.

I have heard critics, for want of something better to say, express the opinion that he is a finer painter than artist. If they have any doubt upon the subject, let them go to Boston, and if teachable, they will learn there that Sargent is not only a rare artist, but a poet and an architect.

Before leaving Boston City I received a call from Mrs. Bancroft, an old lady of eighty, with whom I made friends. She was extremely clever, and when she said I had both grace and genius I thought her an excellent judge! She told me I looked tired, and when we said good-bye, she gave me a bunch of wonderful flowers.

We motored from Boston to Worcester in the Fullers' car, and dined with Mr. and Mrs. Charles M. Thayer, and after an excellent dinner in good company, I delivered a lecture in the private house of Mr. and Mrs. Washburn, at which there were no reporters. Having implored my fellow guests at dinner to interrupt me in the drawing room—as I had never addressed this kind of party before—we opened a sort of debate which I thoroughly enjoyed. I doubt if any English audience, unless of old friends, would have asked such clever and amusing questions, and I knew as I answered back, by the feeling of life and laughter, that it had been a success, and went to bed without remembering the New York lady who had had enough of me.

IV.
UNRESPONSIVE PHILADELPHIA

SERMON ON LIFE AS A TRAINING SCHOOL—MARGOT'S
ENGLISH NOT UNDERSTOOD IN PHILADELPHIA—MRS.
CORNELIUS VANDERBILT'S BAL POUDRÉ—PRAISE FROM
HEYWOOD BROUN

ON Sunday, the 15th of February, Mr. and Mrs. Harry White took me to St. Bartholomew's, a modern church of great beauty. Dr. Parkes, a man of authority and eloquence, preached from the fourth chapter of Galatians, verse 6:

"And because ye are sons, God has sent forth the Spirit of His Son into your hearts."

I did not need to be a Scotch woman to listen to the sermon that he preached. He said that we were fellow students graduating from a great university, joined in the son-ship of Christ, and that we should cultivate a spiritual fellowship with man, since the highest personality could never develop by itself. That our names were entered at our baptism; we received our first diplomas at our confirmation; and the object and mission of the Church was to guide or coach us for the various tests that life would demand from us; and that we should always do what we could to help one another.

As I listened to the rector, knowing how easy I had found it in life to love and care for other people, I wondered how many things I had left undone, and what examination I could pass if suddenly called upon to compete. Haunted from early youth by the transitoriness and pathos of life, I was aware that it was not enough to say, "I am doing no harm," I ought to be testing myself daily, and asking what I was really achieving.

My attention having strayed from the sermon, I was glad to have it recalled by hearing Dr. Parkes say that most people preferred the jazz, the vaudeville, or the movies to the Church.

He said that he would step down for a moment into the pews and ask the pulpit why the services were conventional, monotonous and uninspiring; why the clergy gave unsuitable moral advice, warning the congregation of dangers to which they were not exposed; expressing opinions on politics which they did not share; and convincing them at the end of a tedious service that under no circumstances would they go oftener to church than they could possibly help.

"I will now return to the pulpit," he said; and I listened with close attention.

It was true, the Church was often dull; but the attitude of the congregation was wrong. They ought not to depend upon perpetual entertainment. People went to church for various reasons. Some from habit, some to set a good example, and a few with a yearning hope that they might hear something to heal their tortured minds; something to reassure them that since Jesus wept, He could not be far from those who mourned. Few men were orators, and what filled the churches were the sermons. People would tell you the service was enough, but it obviously was not; or the churches would be crowded every Sunday.

"I have no doubt," he continued, "that I could entertain you for a time; so could the choir and the fine organ, but I feel this would be wrong; it would be taking away from the meaning of the service, and the spiritual fellowship of man. Everyone ought to go to church, as otherwise the churches would cease to exist, and the most irreligious of men could hardly desire this. One day some young prophet or great disciple of Christ might come among us and find no place from where he could speak to the people, and no assemblage that he could address."

I went back to the hotel profoundly impressed by what I had heard and not in the humour to be interviewed by a Philadelphian reporter who was waiting to see me; but I found Mr. V. Hostetter both understanding and intelligent.

* * * * * * *

The next day I went to Philadelphia. The unresponsiveness of my large audience was more than made up for by the kindness of my chairman, Mr. George Gibbs, the hospitality of Mr. and Mrs. Thomas Ridgeway, and the friendliness of the reporters. I doubt if my English was understood, in spite of being informed that I could be heard plainly from the gallery. Except at my first lecture—when I could not stand—I have had no difficulty in making myself heard.

* * * * * * *

On my return to New York, after dining in bed, I joined my daughter at a *bal poudré* given by Mrs. Cornelius Vanderbilt, a clever New

York hostess who thinks nothing of entertaining a hundred and fifty people at lunch, tea or dinner.

One of the noticeable differences between fashion in England and America, is that what might appear to the uninitiated as an almost exaggerated display of hospitality, is as *chic* here as it might be thought over-done in London. American hostesses are also very particular as to precedence: who sits next to whom, or goes in first, second or third. I must confess to being remiss in these ways, and when an American lady at one of these dinners asked me if I minded my daughter, Elizabeth Bibesco, going in or out—I forget which it was—in front of me, I imagined she was joking. I disconcerted a reporter when he asked me if I knew all the British aristocracy, by saying that alas! I did not, but that my maid did.

Nothing could have been prettier than the Vanderbilt ball. I look forward to seeing the house of my kind hosts under more normal conditions, but I could see at a glance that it is not only full of rare and valuable objects, but is really striking. The reception rooms, concert hall, and ballrooms were crowded with fashion and beauty. I gazed about to see if I could find anyone I knew. My eye fell upon my daughter Elizabeth, who in her black velvet Aubrey Beardsley dress was among the prettiest women in the room.

After trying unsuccessfully to detain my beloved friend Colonel House—who hates parties—I caught sight of Mr. Balfour looking young and happy. In spite of the admiring throng by whom he was surrounded I skirmished through, and, taking him by the arm, engaged him in private conversation. Being incapable of flattery, I told him with what extraordinary ability he had represented Great Britain at the Washington Conference; how glad we all were that he had been selected; and how enchanted I was to see him. With the dazzling charm that never deserts him he asked me searching questions as to how my lectures were progressing, and implored me not to tire myself.

I answered that I was always over-tired, but said with truth that neither he nor I would ever grow old.

No one can say that Mr. Balfour does not care for power and politics, but a certain detachment has prevented him from growing old, and by what means I cannot discover, he never appears to be bored in society; it is this, I think, that keeps him young.

I know something about youth, as the Tennants are a race apart; not because we are specially clever, learned, famous, or amusing, but because we have no age. I have been told by gypsies, palmists, phrenologists and other swindlers many senseless and incompatible things, but upon two matters they all agreed. They said I would always be young enough to make love and inspire it, and that I was unmercenary and of a kindly disposition.

In these ways I resemble my father. Sleepless, irritable, impatient, and interested, he could skip and dance at the age of sixty better than most young men in their teens, and his last beautiful daughter was born when he was eighty. This is not entirely physical: it comes no doubt from vitality, but it is also a mixture of moral and intellectual temperament, and, above all things, the power to admire, without which Wordsworth says we cannot live.

After talking to Mr. Balfour, my host Mr. Vanderbilt—a man of character, who cares little for entertainments—showed me his bedroom and his library.

The morning after the ball I contracted a chill which filled me with despair. Having to lecture that afternoon (my fifth in America and second in New York), it was vital to remove the unfortunate impression that sitting down and reading about horses had created upon my first appearance. Unless my secretary cuts out and pins upon my letters press criticisms of myself, I do not look at them, and I had hardly been aware of the severity with which I had been taken to task the day after my first lecture. People are too strong and busy in New York City to notice if you are ill or not; they have paid their dollars and are not likely to listen to what bores them; they wanted a little local gossip about my husband, Mr. Lloyd George, or Princess Mary's trousseau. I did not mind the abuse as I am press-proof, but I did not want to disappoint my manager, Mr. Lee Keedick, a competent, kind man, quite unmercenary, and interested in his client's success, as much from an artistic as a business point of view; or my secretary, Mr. Horton, with whom I have contracted a lasting friendship.

Knowing that I had to speak not only that afternoon but the next night at Brooklyn, I reassured them by saying that in spite of my chill I was going to stand, walk about and amuse the audience by stories of Gladstone, Tennyson, Kitchener, politics, duels and drink. I did not add that I was so nervous that I would have to hold my head up high as, if I dropped it, I would certainly collapse.

My dear friend, Mr. Paul Cravath, in introducing me, made an admirable speech and was more than helpful and encouraging.

I wish I could remember and write down what my chairmen say of me or of my husband, but I am far too anxious to listen, and a cannon ball going off would not prevent me from struggling to remember my speech, in spite of knowing that "Ladies and Gentlemen" will be as far as my memory will take me.

When I stood up, after bowing with challenging languor, I spoke in a slow and deliberate manner which seemed as if it came from another person. I never looked at my notes until the end of the lecture, and after I sat down the audience was enthusiastic. My son-in-law, Prince Bibesco, a man of acute and artistic observation, congratulated me warmly, and speechless with exhaustion I went to bed.

The next morning my chairman sent me the following review out of the *World*: "It Seems to Me," by HEYWOOD BROUN.

"The platform manner of Margot Asquith fills us with envy. We wish we could talk as she does, casually leaning against a table. We must confess to a limitless admiration for her technique. No visiting English author in many seasons has seemed to us so entirely at home as was Mrs. Asquith yesterday afternoon on the stage of the New Amsterdam Theatre. Her utterance is crisp and clear, she is never under the necessity of digging in her heels and shouting. As her point approaches she swings into it, facing the audience square and standing straight. We admired her versatility of delivery. There ought to be many clients eager to be tutored by Mrs. Asquith in the art of public speaking."

If I could have met Mr. Broun that day my gratitude might have made me feel well, but I had a temperature and my daughter having contracted influenza, we were kept in bed and a trained nurse was sent to us by Dr. Eglee.

* * * * * * *

On the eighth I spoke in Brooklyn, where, wrapped up in blankets, I was accompanied in the motor by my doctor. I remained in bed until the 12th, when I made my last appearance in New York. By then I had become quite fashionable, and largely thanks to Mr. Heywood Broun, I received over eighty letters a day, flowers, music, books, and poems. My daughter Elizabeth's illness took away all my joy, and had it not been for her husband and my cousin, Nan Tennant, illness and exhaustion would have tempted me to break my contract.

V.
THE WHITE HOUSE AND WASHINGTON

PRESIDENT HARDING EASY TO TALK TO—MARGOT
EXPLAINS ENGLISH POLITICS—CHATS WITH WOODROW
WILSON—IMPRESSED BY AMBASSADOR JUSSERAND

I arrived at Washington on the 13th alone and spoke the same afternoon.

A Washington audience does not deafen you with applause, but Mr. Thomas Hard, my chairman, was so appreciative that he seemed to set the fashion to laugh and cheer and all went well.

On the following morning I went by appointment at 10.30 to see President Harding. After driving to several wrong doors at the White House I was shown into an ante-room full of press-men talking and smoking round an open fire. The President's secretary was extremely courteous, and I was not kept waiting. Ushered into Mr. Harding's fine circular room we shook hands and sat down. A large black and tan Airedale terrier sniffed round my skirts, and was ordered to sit in a chair by his master. President Harding has a large bold head with well-cut features and an honest, fearless address. He is tall, perfectly simple, and extraordinarily easy and pleasant to talk to. He told me he also had lectured and gave me an account of how lecturing had first started in America. There was a sort of club or society which began round Lake Chautauqua and spread all over the country. It was the only way that either pleasure or information could reach distant and dreary little towns inhabited by thousands of men and women who had neither the fortune or opportunity to meet famous people. While he was telling me this I looked at the big writing table in front of him. I noticed a faded photograph of an extremely pretty, refined, middle-aged woman, and a framed engraving of George Washington; on the top of a book case I observed an interesting print of Abraham Lincoln. A fire in an open grate and large windows looking out upon a garden with trees completed the room.

Our talk was interrupted by a secretary asking the President to speak on the telephone, and he left me after a courteous apology.

On his return he found me looking at the photograph on his table, and informed me that it was his mother. We spoke of Arthur Balfour and I told him how pleased my husband and all of us in England were that he had been able to go to Washington; that his quick mind, fine intellectual manners, and lack of insularity gave him an unrivalled understanding. The President responded with genuine warmth.

"I am very glad," he said, "that he attended our Conference. As you are aware, Mrs. Asquith, he was known and liked here before the Conference, and I can only say that he has added two hundred per cent to his former popularity by the patience, tact, straightforwardness and ability he showed throughout our proceedings."

He talked to me about the political situation in England, and asked when I thought there would be a general election. I told him that the Coalition Liberals were the ambitious, paying guests in a Conservative Palace (or words to that effect); that in their recent attempt to force a general election they had tried to purchase the Palace, but that to their surprise and annoyance Sir George Younger—the keeper of the Tory purse, and manager of their party—had, with a courage undreamt of by his flock, put a veto upon this; and in a polite and public letter given the Coalition Liberals notice to quit. This independent action upset the influential Downing Street press, entertained the Free Liberals, and bewildered the docile Conservatives. The latter having no Prime Minister of their own, are not only deeply indebted to Mr. Lloyd George for all he has done for them, but are committed to his leadership by the mutual bargain of the Kaiser-coupon election.

I told him I had no notion when the election might be sprung upon us, nor could anyone foresee its result, but that if there were many Sir George Youngers in the Conservative Party it was just possible that the Coalition might collapse.

We spoke of the Genoa Conference. I said that frankly I was tired of Government by conference: that, starting from the fatal one at Versailles, to the futile one at Cannes, they had been a source of mischief, misunderstanding and recrimination; and that the only one at which the truth had been faced, discussed and spread was his own at Washington. I tried to give him some idea of the effect that Mr. Hughes's opening speech upon disarmament had produced in our country, adding how profoundly sorry I felt for France. Our "Hang-the-Kaiser," "Search the German pockets," election of 1918, backed as it was by the whole Conservative party, had taken in the French public; and added that half the irascibility, temper and suspicion which we were witnessing in Paris to-day arose from a feeling that they had been cheated. I said with all the earnestness that I could command that neither the Liberal party, my husband, or anyone else in England intended to quarrel with France; that it was equally clear that this view was held in America, and therefore vital for the peace of the world that we should try and understand one another and keep together.

He was eloquent in his agreement, told me how devoted he was to the French people; and added that he felt quite sure the misunderstandings would gradually pass away.

After signing and giving me a facsimile copy of the message which he had delivered at the close of the Washington Conference, we parted.

I went to the Rock Creek Cemetery with my cousin, Nan Tennant, to see the Adams tomb by St. Gaudens. It is a great work, and clutches at your heart. I sat for some time on the circular marble seat and looked at the beautiful bronze statue. It reminded me of the lines in Richard II:

> "Oh! but they say the tongues of dying men
> Enforce attention, like deep harmony."

Although the hooded and austere figure takes you far away from all that moves, and is an emblem of Death, the deep and pitying eyes speak to those who will listen both of Love and of Hope. I thought as I looked at it, what a transfiguring effect a statue like that might have, could it be removed to Paris or Berlin.

In the afternoon I visited ex-President Wilson. His wife greeted me with kindness and affection, and immediately showed me into the library where her husband was sitting erect upon a chair near the bookshelves. His eye was bright, his mind clear, and no one looking at his distinguished face could have imagined that he was ill. I could not conceal my emotion when I told him how often we had thought of him. He seemed hopeful about himself, and said he had still much to do, as there was a stern fight in front of him. He asked me if I did not think things were looking better for my husband and "your great party"; adding how closely, and with what hope he and others were watching the present political situation in England. I told him that he had had the one fine idea, and that all the world was fumbling to follow in its track; adding that the League of Nations was applauded upon every Liberal platform. He made me promise to go and see him on my return to Washington, and after a short conversation

17

about nothing in particular, the fear of tiring him made me get up and say good-bye.

I went on to the French Embassy where I spent over an hour with my old friend M. Jusserand. I found him very unhappy: and when he discussed with frankness and without exaggeration the feelings that were animating Paris, I thought he made out an excellent case for what appears, for the moment, to be a lack of reason in his compatriots. He showed me what Lord Lee had said on Naval Limitation in December at Washington, where he misquoted from Captain Castex's French articles on submarine warfare, actually omitting from the context *"ainsi raisonnent les Allemands"*, which surprised me very much.

I said I was quite sure that there had been some mistake, and that our Admiralty would instantly offer a public apology if the affair could be brought to their notice; he said that on January 7 the Quai d'Orsay had explained, but that nothing further had passed. That in the same article of which Lord Lee had reversed the meaning, Captain Castex had made pointed allusion *"au rôle de salubrité politique, sauvant la liberté du monde, joué par la Grande Bretagne pendant la guerre"*.

I told him that we were too far away to know what was happening, and that it was more than probable that Lord Lee had already apologised; that it was a deplorable blunder as the desire of the French to increase their submarines was understood by the average Englishman to be a menace against Great Britain, as presumably his country would never fight Germany on the sea.

He said that every nation would have to maintain for itself some reserve of force since they had agreed to a large diminution of their armies. I begged him to be patient, and to remember that the 1918 election—so painfully encouraging to the natural desire on the part of the French to pursue a policy of revenge—was not a true reflection of British public opinion; that perhaps we were lacking in imagination but we would never believe in crushing a defeated foe, or trying to keep him down forever. That since no one could get rid of the German race, and France had to remain their neighbour, it appeared to be more sensible to try and discourage hate which was unproductive; and that there was little choice for them unless their intention was to prepare slowly and steadily for another war. He disclaimed all idea of revenge, pointing out that we were an island without frontiers, and that twice within the recollection of one generation their industrious and arrogant neighbour had not only killed their people, but laid waste their territory, and added that he and his compatriots did not feel their moral and financial sufferings had been treated either with sufficient sympathy or justice.

He argued extremely well, and I felt as I left him that we ought to do everything possible to remove the suspicions, and heal the wounds, of a country at whose side we have fought and died.

I dined that night in a company of fifty at the British Embassy and had some talk with our Ambassador, Sir Auckland Geddes.

VI.
DETROIT AND CHICAGO

GUEST OF WOMEN'S CLUB—VISITS FORD WORKS—LOVELY
MRS. MINOTTO—BONUS AND DISABLED SOLDIERS

THE next morning we left Washington for Detroit, where I met with a warm welcome and lectured with success. I was entertained by the Women's City Club, at whose original invitation I had gone to Detroit. They were interesting women who all had some work of their own to do, and talked to me about serious matters with keenness and freedom. I told them, in saying good-bye, that I had been honoured by meeting them at lunch, and hoped some of them would write when they had time and tell me a little more about their lives.

After lunch we motored in a beautiful Hudson car—lent to us through the kindness of Mr. and Mrs. Chapin who had been introduced to me by my artist friend Nellie Komroff—to the great Ford works at Highland Park. I regret to say I have never understood machinery, and the deafening noise, smell of oil, and endless walking exhausted me. I was also unlucky in finding Mr. Ford away, as I would have much liked to have met him. He is a man who has rendered a great service to his country, as he has put at the disposal of nearly everybody automobiles of low price and high quality.

* * * * * * *

We travelled that night to Columbus in the same sort of horrible train—shaky, hot, and stopping outside before jerking into the stations. Upon our arrival, a stranger came up to us on the platform and said he hoped we would let him take us and our luggage to any place we liked; that he had loved my book and was going to hear my lecture. We were delighted to accept his invitation and were whizzed off to the hotel. Mr. Jeffries, the owner of the motor, was more than kind and enthusiastic. I tried to distinguish his handsome face in a ballroom where I spoke in the evening, but he was in the gallery, and I was too nervous to look much about me.

Ex-Governor Campbell made a witty introductory speech and encouraged my listeners to ask me questions. When it was all over, I was surrounded by various ladies and gentlemen of the audience who introduced themselves and each other to me and asked if I would not eat ices and drink punch, but I was dropping with fatigue and even my handsome friend who was full of congratulations, could not prevent me from staggering off to bed.

I had received a wire from my manager begging me to go by the 7 a.m. train next morning to Chicago in time to see the reporters in the evening. The prospect of this gave me a sleepless night, especially as I was disturbed, first at midnight by a messenger boy with an album which he wished me to sign, and again at two in the morning by the night watchman who said I had neglected to lock my door. I used un-parliamentary language, telling him that nothing would induce me to lock my door, and after an unsuccessful attempt to settle down, I turned on the light and read "If Winter Comes."

The originality and pathos of this wonderful study reduced me to tears and, more dead than alive, at 5.30 a.m. I told my maid I would have my bath.

The reporters at Chicago were very civil and, interspersed with flash-lights, I got through the interviews as well as I could. One of the young ladies, following me to the lift, said:

"I wish you hadn't been so charming and polite. I would like you to have just rushed at me and pulled my hair out so that I could have got the story."

I looked at her in surprise and disgust as Mr. Horton elbowed me into the lift.

I dined that night with a very old friend of mine, Count Minotto, and met the first woman of real beauty that I have seen since I came here. Mrs. Minotto walked into the room with long white arms and a transparently pale face; her dark hair brushed in waves off her forehead was knotted loosely at the back of her neck, and her beautiful eyes glowed with welcome. We talked à trois for three hours and before going away she took me into her night nursery. The nurse woke up, but her lady told her not to move, and after looking at a handsome little boy, she glided to the side of a white cradle. Very tall, in a clinging black crepe dress, I was struck by the beauty of her attitude, and the tenderness of her expression as, leaning across the cot, she removed the coverlet for me to see her little sleeping baby.

I lectured the next night to the biggest and most intelligent audience I had faced since Boston, and when it was over people came on to the stage to congratulate me and ask for my autograph.

On the morning of the 22nd, having asked to see the big Military Hospital, a friend of Mr. Horton's—who had been his secretary during his Foreign Office work in Paris—took us out to see the Speedway Hospital.

We had a long and adventurous drive, skidding in circles on the ice, although we went at an almost funereal pace. Puffs of steam came up from my feet which seemed to emerge from a furnace. Mr. Horton insisted on stopping at a garage for fear the car would catch fire, and our chauffeur in a rough-and-ready manner poured cans of water down the window spaces to do what he could to cool the car.

On arriving at the hospital we were greeted by interviewers and doctors (the latter in khaki),—we had taken with us Miss Allard, a lady reporter of first rate intelligence and fine manners,—and we started to walk round. The military doctor wanted naturally enough to show me the hospital, which I should imagine to be the largest and most perfectly equipped in the world. This solid building extends for over half a mile, and is several storeys high; but I wanted to see the patients, and I loathe long passages and operating paraphernalia. With difficulty I was finally permitted to see the wounded.

It is difficult to make conversation with tired men acclimatized to pain and bed, but I was glad to meet and talk to them.

I have a feeling, which may be wrong, that they are not getting the attention they deserve in this country of money and movies, but the hospital was magnificent, and there at any rate, they are treated with efficiency and understanding.

Perhaps I am not competent to judge, but from what I have observed, the men who fought in the war—many of whom have been either permanently disabled or financially handicapped—are in danger of being forgotten, not by the Government either in the States or any other part of the world, but by the private individual.

The bonus over here, even if it passes, can never be an excuse for the rich and leisured not to go among the wounded either at their homes or in the hospitals. Gassed, crippled and shell-shocked, their outlook at the best can but be forlorn, and I am haunted by a fear that in the hustle of life and what is erroneously called the "return to normality," the crippled and wounded are neglected. It is understandable that men in business should want to make money, but business principles should not be mainly the reflection of personal interests and you may pay too high a price for making your fortune.

Excepting for myself I saw no stranger in the crowded wards of this immense hospital, and from answers to my questions, I do not think it is the practice among women over here to visit them.

VII.
PITTSBURGH AND ROCHESTER

MEETS AN INTERESTING REPORTER—COMPLIMENTS FROM
DR. HOLLAND—PULLMAN CAR INCONVENIENCES—
MARGOT SEES HER FIRST FLAPPER

AFTER travelling all night in a train that would not be tolerated for a day in England, we jolted into Pittsburgh at 6.30 a.m. on the morning of the 23rd. Reporters and photographers waited in the sitting room to see me after breakfast and, giddy from the journey, I put my feet upon a sofa and awaited their intelligent questions.

I spoke to three women and one man. The women asked me if I did not think they were advancing rapidly as a nation; I answered that no doubt interest in international politics was making them less provincial, and with their vitality, intelligence, and resources, their country was bound to exercise enormous political influence in the future, if it was not already doing so. I observed the male reporter demurred to this; he said that the men of ideas and captains of industry were fighting each other all the time, and that the American press pandered to the public taste by keeping them in ignorance of the truth. The ladies challenged this and, addressing him as "Bruce," asked if he thought they did not revere their great men and all that was worth while; adding that they were a young and free nation and, if anything, going far too fast.

Appealing to me, I felt obliged to say I thought they were the most genuine and hospitable of people, but that in spite of being always in a hurry I had found them slow; nor could I honestly say I thought them a free nation, I was heartily supported by the solitary man, who asked the ladies where they had observed either the great men, or the reverence; he said that materialism was sapping the soul of America, that their men of intellect were choked out, and in an aside to me in French, while the photographers were taking flash-lights, begged me to let him stay on after the ladies had departed. I assented, and when the oft repeated enquiry as to what I thought of "flappers" came up, I listened with absent mind and without committing myself to a subject that, while disturbing to the morals of the female questioners, bores me to such an extent that I almost scream when it is mentioned.

After the ladies had gone Mr. Horton returned with "Bruce." He was the most interesting reporter that I have met up till now.

He said he did not know what had happened to the spirit of his fellow-countrymen. Whether it was from temporary restlessness—following the chaos of present conditions—or from a native and ingrained lack of reflection, but that jazz, hustle and headlines were killing the soul of the American people.

"There is a perpetual antagonism between the machine, the press, the money makers, and those who are groping in the darkness to be free. When they see the Light, and know the Truth, it will be as bad over here as it is in Russia to-day, and, Mrs. Asquith," he added, "why should this be? We have men of ideas, and are young and keen; why must what is fine be inarticulate? You won't believe me, but in this very hotel I heard one man say to another:

"'I never read a line that is not going to profit me in commerce.'

"Imagine, after these five years of anguish all over the world, that such a thing could be said! I'm a poor man, never likely to arrive, but I would rather starve than say a thing like that."

"Have you read 'If Winter Comes'?" I asked.

He answered that he had, and told me he had been deeply moved over it; but did I believe that such a man as Mark Sabre could ever exist; did I not think he had emanated from a sensitive and creative power, but was not quite a real being. I replied that it was just because Mark Sabre was so human, and made by God as well as Hutchinson, that the book was great.

"If we cared enough, we all have it in us to develop some of Sabre's qualities, but we must be equally independent of public opinion, equally tolerant and, above all, equally selfless and loving," I said.

"You may be right, but what good, after all, did it do him?"

"Of course," I replied, "if every time we do or say the right thing we expect to succeed, matters would be very simple. It is because we are always meeting with rebuffs that life is so complicated. We must peg away doing what we can; fundamentally humble and despising popular opinion. Believe me, you are not the only country exposed to the temptations you speak of. We can only overcome these eternal inequalities by pity and self-sacrifice, and of this we have been given an immortal example."

He got up, and, shaking me firmly by the hand, said:

"It was just as well that Christ was crucified when He was, for He would not long have survived the hate and antagonism that His ideas provoked among the conventional, the successful, and the governing classes."

In the afternoon I was taken over the Carnegie Buildings. By the kindness of Mr. Church I was rolled about in a chair, and enjoyed the most wonderful institution of its sort that exists. Dr. Holland, who informed me that he was not only acquainted with all my literary friends in England, but with most of the crowned heads of Europe, accompanied us. Stuffed animals in huge glass cases do not usually attract me, but at the Carnegie Institute they are presented with such life-like skill that I begged to be introduced to the man who had arranged them. He was brought down in a lift from his work, and after shaking him warmly by the hand, I told him how proud I was to meet so great an artist.

Dr. Holland, my chairman of that night, was kind enough to give me the rough copy of his introductory speech:

"Ladies and Gentlemen, neighbours, and friends," he said.

"Written history has been called a 'tissue of lies.' Most historians, like portrait painters, feel it to be their duty to impart to the characters whom they are describing a glamour, which in many cases is more or less superhuman or super-diabolical as the case may be, and to represent circumstances as they happened in the light of the preternatural. Now and then there arises a writer who is gifted with the quality to see things as they really are, and who, to use a current phrase, 'calls a spade a spade.' In an age of pretence, it is to many more or less shocking to have such persons take up the pen and, with frankness born of native honesty, tell the truth as he or she may distinctly perceive it. Society is so used to 'diplomatic courtesies' that when the truth-teller arrives, society 'takes a fit,' seeing its illusions vanish. Its would-be idols which have been proclaimed as made of pure gold, are found to be gilded clay, its devils not so devilish after all, and the daring act of the truth-teller is vigorously denounced by an age which calls for nothing but compliments.

"We have all read, at least I have, with great appreciation, coupled with no small degree of amusement, Mrs. Margot Asquith's 'Autobiography.' I particularly enjoyed it because it gave her impressions of many people whom I have met and known.

"Mrs. Asquith is the wife of the great man who was the prime minister of England at the outbreak of the World War. She is here to-day in a city which bears the name of that prime minister of England who held the helm of state during the Napoleonic wars.

"I have the honour of presenting Mrs. Margot Asquith, wife of the Right Honourable Herbert Henry Asquith. She is one of the most famous women of England."

Hampered by the knowledge that we were to catch the night train to Rochester, and inexperienced in timing what I have to say, I found when I sat down that I had cut my lecture short by half an hour. To make up for this, and encouraged by people in the front row reaching up to shake my hand, I invited them to come on to the platform. They trooped up in large numbers and I held an informal reception which met with unexpected success.

We drove in silence to the station. I had a conviction which my secretary did not attempt to contradict that I had been a failure. Mr. Horton said he feared the news of my curtailed lecture might reach the influential press and prejudice those who might want to hear me in the towns in which I was booked to speak. Knowing in my heart that I had on every occasion received more praise than I deserved, and being of a temperament that is not knocked out by failure, I tried to cheer him up while the nigger was arranging my bed, but without the smallest success.

The trains, both in the States and in the Dominion, have every fault; those in Canada being even worse than in the United States. If you travel by day you are one of twenty-four men, women, and children who sit on hard revolving chairs eyeing one another. You cannot stretch your limbs, or smoke a cigarette, and while your ears are deafened by shrieking babies, your legs are scorched by boiling pipes. If you are rich enough, you may get a drawing room, but they do not have them on every train. When you travel by night men and women are on top of one another, buttoned behind an avenue of green cotton curtains. You cannot get your hot water bottles filled, or have tea in the morning. While staggering to your private berth between the leaps of the locomotive you are lucky if you do not fall over the protruding feet of your fellow travellers, or find yourself sitting on the face of a sleeping lady lying *perdue* behind the hangings. Privacy is unknown, and though I have travelled for thousands of miles I have not yet met the train that, unless you have the balance of a ballet girl, will not give you concussion of the spine or brain.

After a sleepless night we arrived at Rochester where I seized the morning papers. Thanks to a charming reporter, Mr. C. M. Vining, who had come a long way to hear me speak at Pittsburgh, I had an excellent review.

My stay was so short at Rochester, where I lectured under the auspices of the Press Club, that I had no time to form any impressions of the place, but the people were all very good to me.

On the 26th we met Mr. Horton's mother at Buffalo, a refined, charming, old lady, who travelled in the train to Toronto with us.

Meeting Mr. Vining in the passage I thought if I brought him into our drawing room it would give my secretary an opportunity of speaking to his mother, and invited him to join us. We had an excellent talk and I told him that, for the first time in my life, I had seen a "flapper." While waiting in the sunny street outside Buffalo station, I had seen two young, short-skirted giggling girls, walking with their admirers who were armed with kodaks. One of the young men threw a girl over his shoulder who stretched out her legs while the other photographed her. I added that, while praying that I would never again be interviewed upon the subject, I would be in a better position to answer my ardent questioners in the future.

VIII.
TORONTO AND MONTREAL

MARGOT TELLS A MARK TWAIN STORY—CAPTURES TORONTO AUDIENCE; KISSES CHARWOMAN—MONTREAL LADIES QUELLING AND CRITICAL

THAT evening we arrived at Toronto and I lectured on the 29th. My chairman, the Rev. Byron Stauffer, made a wonderful speech, and I was listened to by an attentive and intelligent audience.

I find Prohibition a fruitful topic of discussion.

For the information of anyone who may think, as I did, that drink has decreased, and that in consequence everyone over here is wise, sober and happy, I can only say the reverse is the truth.

I cannot write of the poorer classes, on whom, in any case, the law is hard, but among the rich I do not suppose there was ever so much alcohol concealed and enjoyed as at the present moment in America. Young men and maidens, who before this exaggerated interference would have been content with the lightest of wines, think it smart to break the law every day and night of their lives. I related to my audience that Mr. Clemens, (better known as Mark Twain), had taken me in to dinner many years ago at the house of a namesake of mine (Mrs. Charles Tennant, whose daughter Dorothy married Stanley) and had told me of a great American temperance orator who, having exercised his voice too much, had asked the chairman to provide milk instead of water at his meeting. Turning to the Rev. Byron Stauffer, who is a great temperance preacher—of which I was unaware—I said,

"The chairman—probably a kind man like my own—put rum into the milk, and when the orator, pausing in one of his most dramatic periods, stopped to clear his throat, he drained the glass, and putting it down, exclaimed,

"Gosh! what cows!"

I went on to tell of a lady who was letting her house, and, after instructing the auctioneer as to the value of her chairs, furniture and china, had left him in the dining room where the side-board had several bottles of wine and whiskey on it. She waited for a long time hoping he would return to show her the inventory, but as he did not appear she went into the dining room where she found him drunk upon the floor. She looked at the paper he held in his hand and read,

"To one revolving carpet."

Not wishing to repeat the mistake I had made in Pittsburgh, I spoke for an hour and fifteen minutes, longer than which no one can be expected to endure, and as we had some time before catching a midnight train, I invited my audience on to the stage. At this the platform was stormed, and I was seized by hands and arms, showered with compliments and, never at any time a robust figure, so crowded and crushed that I felt suffocated. My reverend chairman did his best, but it was not until Mr. Horton, in a voice of thunder, begged them not to mob me as I had to catch a train, that I was allowed to move. They all rushed to the stage door shouting,

"We think you are wonderful!" "Why can't you stay with us?" "You must come back!" "You're perfectly lovely!" etc.

We had to lock one of the doors of the green room, but while I was given brandy, and congratulated by my chairman and his family, a very old charwoman peeped in at another entrance, saying with emotional timidity,

"Excuse me, but though I am only a poor old woman who sweeps the stage, I would like to shake hands with you. The last famous person that I spoke to was Mme. Calvé, over whom we were all crazy; I may say she let me kiss her hand."

I turned and kissed the old lady on both her wrinkled cheeks, at which she blest me and burst into tears. I felt like doing the same, but was steadied by the presence of my jolly chairman and his relations. It was with a feeling of tense gratitude that I heard the announcement of our car. Clinging to the arm of my secretary I swayed through an enthusiastic crowd gathered on the pavement. They were cheering, waving handkerchiefs, and throwing up their hats. Half of the audience appeared to have waited and collected round our motor, and we had the greatest difficulty in reaching it. Knowing that this sort of thing will probably never happen to me again, and with a touch of vanity that I seldom feel, I wished my husband had been there to witness my unexpected triumph.

Upon our arrival in Montreal I saw the reporters, and in the afternoon I made my speech.

I was introduced at His Majesty's Theatre, by a delightful woman, a relative of the well known Lady Drummond—Mrs. Huntley

Drummond—and spoke to a lady-like assemblage in a blizzard of draughts. To quote my beloved and early friend, Mr. John Hay, "I chill like mutton gravy," and had it not been for my chairwoman who left the stage to bring me my fur boa, I must have contracted a permanent catarrh which would have reduced my voice to a whisper. I was relieved—a feeling which I thought the audience shared—when my lecture was over.

His Majesty's Theatre is an odious place to speak in, and whether from the fatigue of a night journey, or the refinement of my female listeners, I formed an unfavourable impression of the intellectual manners and vitality of Montreal. When I retired to the wings of the stage I pointed out to Mrs. Drummond two women in the front row whose attention and enthusiasm had made all the difference to me during the lecture. One had a masculine face, with an earnest and beautiful expression, and her neighbour was a lovely creature.

"Those," she said, "are Mrs. Hayter Reed and Mrs, Lawford."

Luckily for me they came up to the green room, accompanied by Oswald Balfour—Military Secretary to the Governor General—followed by an old man with a huge bag of golf clubs, and several other friendly people. The old man showed me a photograph of my father given to him on the links at Carnoustie, which touched me deeply; and my friends in the front row, after embracing me on both cheeks, assured me they had been thrilled by all that I had said, and only longed to see more of me. Mrs. Drummond—a woman of rare intellect—joined in this praise, and after Oswald—whose mother, Lady Francis Balfour, is the finest woman speaker in England—said that my voice-production, general manner and delivery were professional, I retired from a quelling and critical company.

My host that night was Sir Frederick Taylor, and I met Lady Drummond and Mr. Charles Hosmer in his beautiful house. He was more than kind to me, and I found that they knew most of my personal friends. When Lady Drummond said that I had a beautiful smile, and the papers that I had a golden voice, I felt less exhausted on my journey to Ottawa.

No one who has not been on tour in America can imagine the fatigue of crowded elevators, shaky trains, and perpetual travelling.

IX.

IN CANADA'S CAPITAL

APATHY AND BREEDING OF OTTAWA'S AUDIENCE —
INTIMATE TALK WITH PREMIER MACKENZIE KING — THE
STATUE OF "SIR GALAHAD" AND ITS STORY

WE arrived at Ottawa on the first of March and lunched with Sir George Perley and his wife (who had befriended me upon the *Carmania*). Lady Perley is a treasure of kindness and understanding, and nothing I could ever do will repay her.

At lunch I met Mr. Meighen and the Canadian Premier. In inviting the defeated Minister and Mr. MacKenzie King to meet each other, my hostess reminded me of the early days where in my father's house Mr. Gladstone, Lord Randolph Churchill, and other Cabinet Ministers of rival parties met and discussed politics.

I was grateful to Mr. Meighen for the cordiality with which he greeted me, as the inventive Canadian press had added impromptu reflections of their own to what I had said of him. I sat next to Mr. MacKenzie King, but as we had no opportunity of private conversation, he invited me to go to his house for supper after the lecture.

The capital of the Dominion is a beautiful town, wonderfully situated, and in spite of being covered with snow, was alive and radiant with spangles and sunshine.

A greater contrast to the audiences of New York, Boston, Chicago, Rochester or Toronto, than the one I addressed in Ottawa could hardly be imagined, and I recognised some of the apathy and breeding which had characterised my listeners in Montreal. I was introduced to several select and fashionable people and one gentleman gave me an inventory of our British aristocracy, most of whom he had known and stayed with. I felt like putting my arm on his shoulder and saying with sympathy, "Never mind!" but refrained. When the lecture was over I motored to Mr. King's private apartments.

The Canadian Premier is a man after my own heart; shrewd, straight, modest and cultured. I was surprised to find how much he knew, not only of the political situation in England, but of the chief characters concerned in it. After discussing Mr. Lloyd George, Mr.

Churchill, Lord Birkenhead, and Mr. Bonar Law's Canadian friend Lord Beaverbrook, we talked of Sir Wilfred Laurier, President Harding, and Mr. Hughes. He spoke with genuine admiration of Mr. Hughes's speech and the Washington Conference and agreed with me in condemnation of the many futile confabulations that had preceded it.

He asked me about the Irish Free State and Labour conditions in England. As he had settled most of the Canadian strikes he was interested in unemployment.

I told him the "land fit for heroes to live in" was a less fashionable resort than was generally supposed; and that thanks to the policy of "official reprisals" the ground had not been prepared in a manner to encourage either Craig or Collins to place implicit confidence in the Coalition. He told me that reprisals had come as a shock to all thoughtful people; and, pointing to a fine Italian picture of Our Lord hanging on the wall, asked me if His life had captivated me as much as it had him.

I said that following in His steps appeared to me to be the only chance we could ever have of acquiring that purity of heart which would enable us to see God; and walked up to examine the picture.

It does not take a long sojourn in Canada to prophecy that Mr. MacKenzie King will need all his courage and independence if he is to stand up to the hostility of his Conservative and fashionable opponents; but if he can make himself known to thinking men his administration ought to prove successful.

The next day I was again the guest of the premier, and met one of the two sitting members for Ottawa,—Mr. Hal McGiverin; the Hon. Dr. Henri Beland (Minister of Soldiers Civil Re-establishment), who had been a distinguished physician in Belgium when the war broke out. He wrote "A Thousand and One Days in a Berlin Prison" after having been taken prisoner by the Germans and confined for over three years. During his incarceration his wife died in Belgium, and he was not permitted to attend her death-bed or her funeral. The Hon. George Graham, Minister of Militia, whose only son was killed in the War; the Hon. Sir Lomar Gouin, Minister of Justice, and the only other lady, Mrs. G. B. Kennedy, made up our luncheon party. We had general conversation, which my stepson Raymond once described as a series of "ugly rushes and awkward pauses", but on this occasion it was successful, as we discussed among other subjects politics and literature.

I asked my neighbour what the statue was which commanded such a wonderful view near the Houses of Parliament. He said it was "Sir Galahad," and had been erected in memory of a deed of heroism, and had no other inscription upon it. He told me a young man called Henry Albert Harper was skating with a friend when he observed a couple in front of him disappear into the river at a sudden break in the ice. He sent his companion to the shore for help, and lying down, stretched out his walking stick to see if the lady in the water, or her friend, could catch hold of it. Seeing that this was impossible, as they neither of them could reach it, he rose to his feet and took off his coat. The other skaters implored him not to attempt to rescue them as it meant certain death.

"What else can I do?" said young Harper, and plunged into the icy current. Their dead bodies were found the next morning.

Hearing that Mr. MacKenzie King had written a memoir of Harper—who had been his greatest friend—I begged him to give me a copy of it. He sent it to me with his autograph in it, and asked me to sign his volume of my own autobiography. I was truly sorry to say good-bye to the Canadian Premier.

We returned to Montreal the next morning where I found my room a garden of flowers given to me by Mrs. Reed, Mrs. Lawford and Lady Drummond. I addressed a ballroom that night full of empty chairs and chandeliers, but was consoled by my flowers, and the ladies with whom I afterwards went to supper; and I hope and think I have made lasting friendships with Mrs. Hayter Reed and Mrs. Lawford.

Mrs. Reed told me that the little son of friends of hers who had always refused to meet a Jew, had disconcerted them, one day, by saying in a reproachful voice,

"Mother, you never told me Jesus Christ was a Jew."

Seeing a distressed expression upon his mother's face, he added consolingly: "But it doesn't matter, since God was a Presbyterian."

Lying awake that night, I wondered what I would have felt had I married a man who had consented to be either Governor General of Canada or Viceroy of India. I can imagine no career, excepting perhaps that of a minor royalty, that I would have minded as much. Not all the great functions, personal prestige, wonderful scenery, pig-sticking in the East, or skating in the Dominion, would make up to me for friendships without intimacy, and grandeur without gaiety. I came to the conclusion that only men of a certain kind of vanity and ambition, or animated by the highest sense of public duty could ever be found to fill these honourable positions.

X.
REFLECTIONS AT LARGE

DRAWBACKS OF AMERICAN JOURNALISM—SENSATIONAL
HEADLINES; FEAR OF THE PRESS—CONTROVERSY ON
PROHIBITION WITH LORD LEE—IMPRESSIONS OF U. S.
SENATE

WE breakfasted at 5.30 a.m. the next morning and arrived at New York at ten that night, to be greeted by a room full of press men. When the female reporters begin by saying to me:

"What, Mrs. Asquith, do you think, with your close acquaintance with the many trends of the working of a woman's mind, of the modern probability etc., etc.," I am reminded of Sir Walter Raleigh's excellent phrase, "Stumbling upwards into vacuity."

One of these eager ladies, checking her more intelligent male companions, said:

"Tell me, Mrs. Asquith, is it not true that you are indifferent to the opinion of any living person and enjoy saying smart and daring things?" I replied:

"Indeed no! I leave that to you."

I told them about MacKenzie King, of whom they had never heard, and what Mr. Horton and I had observed in our travels of the abominable consequences of Prohibition. I said it was a measure of such exaggerated interference with private liberty that no truthful person could call America a free country.

On my arrival I found many letters from England on the political crisis; and if I can judge at such a distance, the Coalition seems doomed.

Believing as I always have in party government as the best solution for democracy, I think Sir George Younger deserves a Victoria Cross, and it will be interesting to see how many of the timid Conservatives will regain sufficient courage to follow him. The mischief that is being made between my husband and Lord Grey leaves me cold.

Their friendship is not of a kind to be easily severed, and the House of Lords and the House of Commons are separate institutions.

Trammelled as I have always been by an unfortunate combination of truthfulness and impatience, and exhausted by the journey of eighteen hours, I was afraid I had been neither genial nor informing to the reporters upon my arrival in New York, but on looking at the papers next morning I found they had treated me with friendliness and courtesy.

Journalism over here is not only an obsession but a drawback that cannot be over-rated. Politicians are frightened of the press, and in the same way as bull-fighting has a brutalising effect upon Spain (of which she is unconscious), headlines of murder, rape, and rubbish, excite and demoralise the American public.

I would like to make it clear that it is not the reporters but the owners of the papers that should be censured. With the exception of a few garrulous and gushing geese, who think it smart to ask pert and meaningless questions, the male reporters that I have met have not only been serious and intelligent, but men with whom I have discussed literature, politics and religion; but it would not pay their editors, I presume, to publish conversations of this character. On the front page of even the best newspapers, paragraph after paragraph is taken up by descriptions in poor English of devastating trivialities. Violent and ignorant young men, or "flappers" — in whom the public here seem to take an unnatural interest — might easily suppose that their best chance of success in life lay in creating a sensation. Of what use can it be to create a sensation? Who profits by it? What influence can this sort of thing have upon the morals of a great and vital nation? If Christ with His warnings against worldliness were to come down to-day, after giving Him one hearing the crowd would not crucify Him, they would shoot Him at sight.

You have only to examine the newspaper comments upon Abraham Lincoln to see that even in those days abuse and misrepresentation were popular. He was persecuted and vilified every day of his life; but, like my husband, he was press-proof.

If editors would only realise it, following public opinion instead of guiding it is ultimately dull, and makes monotonous reading.

In England we are trying to raise our journalistic standards to the level of the United States, but, without claiming undue superiority, I do not think we shall succeed. There is enough common sense among our people to mitigate against any such misfortune, and we have only to recall the general election of 1905-6, when every morning paper in London, except the *Daily News*, was against us, to realise the impotence of the press.

Fear is as unproductive as it is contemptible, and until some big man has the courage to break the power of the press in America, progress will always go beyond civilisation.

* * * * * * *

I motored in evening dress for three hours to a suburb of New York. I am so tired of the abominable trains that an aeroplane or a perambulator would be a relief, and the road to Montclair was full of interest. The sky was throbbing with carmine and gold, and the varying lights of green and white, reflected in a river sentinelled on either side by high black buildings and pointed towers, left an impression on me of Whistler-like beauty.

We dined with excited and hospitable people and I lectured to an enthusiastic audience. I do not know how it is with professional speakers, but with the amateur the chairman and the audience make the speech. The Rev. Swan Wiers introduced me in an address of eloquence for which I thanked him warmly.

I arrived in Providence next day to be interviewed by three young ladies. After the usual questions upon Princess Mary's underwear and the "flappers," one of them said she had come to ask me about England's greatest man. I told her we had so many that I would be grateful if she could indicate the one she meant.

"Will you tell me who your great men are?" she answered.

"Well," I said, "we have Hardy, Kipling, Lord Morley, Lord Grey, Lord Buckmaster, and Mr. Balfour."

"Oh, no!" she replied, "I want to hear all about Lloyd George."

"I fear you will have to read about him yourself," I said, "and if you can wade through the daily columns of films, flappers, murders and headlines, over here, to our anonymous gossip about Downing Street in my country, you may discover what you want to know."

The other ladies intervened when she retorted:

"Then you refuse to tell me?" and as—the electric light having gone out all over the hotel—we were squinting at a single candle, I thought it as well to put an end to their intelligent questions.

The Providence audience consisted mostly of empty chairs, but it was an enormous hall and when the lecture was over a few of the five hundred listeners came up to ask me to sign my name in various albums and on slips of paper. They said:

"You have given us such a wonderful lecture to-night that you must come back here." To which I replied smilingly:

"Never in this world! To speak for an hour and fifteen minutes to people who never clap is like hitting one's head against a wall." At which one of the ladies said:

"You are quite right, Mrs. Asquith, there is great apathy and lack of manners in Providence."

"Why should you clap," I said, "if you are not interested?" At this they all protested.

"We were afraid of missing a word of what we were enjoying," said one charming woman, to which I replied:

"I would have stood as still as a statue if one of you had thought of cheering me!"

We took the midnight train to New York where we arrived at six the next morning, and I felt that I was returning home.

On March 8, the *New York Times* published on its front page:

"LORD LEE DEFENDS AMERICAN YOUNG WOMEN

"Mrs. Asquith's Charges Cruel, Ludicrous, and Untrue!"

"Speaking at the English-speaking Union luncheon, Lord Lee said the statement attributed to the famous country-woman of his now in the United States was as cruel as it was ludicrous and untrue. He added that he could testify from thirty years of personal observation in America, and from reliable information from various quarters; and that he was speaking seriously."

Lord Lee has only got to travel over here for ten days to change his opinion. I, also, am speaking seriously, and am strongly in favour of temperance. Liquor control has been, among many other reforms, the political ambition of my husband ever since he became a Cabinet Minister, but as what is called "the Trade" has the votes and blessing of the Conservative Party in England, all our bills to control it were frustrated by the House of Lords.

We drink less than our forbears, not because we are more moral, but for reasons of health. Our people are fond of sport; and you neither shoot or ride as straight if you indulge in champagne, port, liqueurs, brandies, and other drinks over night.

The first question I was asked when I landed upon American soil was whether I approved of Prohibition. I said I thought it was a fine idea and an example that would ultimately be followed by the whole world; I presumed that light wines and beer would in time modify this somewhat exaggerated measure; but as most of the men convicted of crimes of violence had been proved to be under the influence of liquor, the prisons and asylums would gradually be emptied. I added that many of the famous, as well as young men of promise, and some of the best servants I had known in my life had been ruined by drink, and that it was a subject upon which I felt deeply.

I could see at once that what I said was unpopular, but I repeated the same opinion in all my early lectures, adding that gout, rheumatism, arthritis, and other nervous diseases have been, if not contracted, certainly assisted by alcoholic poisoning inherited from generations of men who drank too much.

A very short visit over here has convinced me that Prohibition, as at present administered, is both "ludicrous and cruel." The well-to-do can get the drinks they want. Young men and women, as well as adults, share with their friends and admirers all the pleasures that go with defying the law. I have no doubt from what I have been told that the power of the Saloon League lobby had to be smashed, and that the men who accomplished it deserve the highest praise, but can anyone truly say the Prohibition law is kept? Are Mr. Volstead or Mr. Pussyfoot Johnson satisfied with the present condition of things in their country?

There is a text in St. John,

"The Truth shall make you free."

There is no lack of truth over here, but there is a lack of freedom, and I think the press which is kept informed of what is going on might do much more than it does with its powers upon this subject.

It cannot be right for young people to see their parents and friends cheating the law every day of their lives. And which of them think of cheering up the poor, who presumably get as tired from their work as the idle get from their pleasures! What I have said upon every platform and which Lord Lee, in a generous desire to defend the youth of this country, denies, is not "cruel, ludicrous, and untrue," but a platitude.

I have received signed letters from every quarter of the country thanking me for expressing my opinion, and will quote from one of them:

"New York City, March 9, 1922.

MADAM,

"If you wish for very substantial proof of the exactitude of your remark that maidens get drunk at dances, all you have to do is to send someone, unobtrusively, to [I am not going to give the name of the place] to obtain from the waiters and waitresses an account of the lamentable condition in which scores of the girls were taken home after two recent balls held in the Hotel — —, one of the most fashionable hotels in the suburbs of New York.

"It was not the fault of the management, and I am told no more dances of the sort will be permitted there.

"I am a very disgusted sister of one of the young girls, and am trying hard to dissuade her from accepting intoxicants at these parties. Yours, etc."

[I will not publish the signature.]

This is only one of many letters I have received on the same subject.

After the *New York Times* had published Lord Lee's statement and I had made my position perfectly clear, I was sent a press cutting, from what paper I do not know.

"Margot Lines Up with Foes of Prohibition: she has swung round to the anti-prohibitionists."

This is characteristic of the inaccuracy of the American press. Editors do not distinguish between half notes and full shouts, but no one need take this seriously as crime and headlines will soon make their readers forget either what Lord Lee has said, or I have controverted.

On the 10th my daughter Elizabeth took me to a fashionable charity fête in a large New York ballroom, where I heard my son-in-law speak for the first time. I envied him his self-possession; for, though I am told that my demeanor does not betray me, I am so nervous before the so-called "lectures" that I eat nothing, and so exhausted after, that the mildest meal gives me indigestion.

Having suffered from audiences that, while more than appreciative, seldom clap, Mrs. Frank Polk and I were determined that Antoine Bibesco should not experience the same embarrassment. Our friendly intentions were frustrated, however, as everything he said was received with enthusiasm. His handsome face and fine manners, and the popularity of his wife (though it is not usual to praise one's daughter) have made them much loved in this hospitable country.

On leaving the entertainment I was way-laid by a female reporter:

"Is it not true that but for his Highness Prince Bibesco you would never have published your diaries, Mrs. Asquith?" she asked. To which I replied:

"I have not published my diaries. I have written the first volume of my autobiography, encouraged by some of my friends—but no one has criticised my literary efforts with more perspicacity and insight than my son-in-law."

"Can you not give me a story for my paper?" she said.

The gallantry of Mr. Nelson Cromwell, and presence of mind of Mrs. Frank Polk rescued me from further conversation.

Mr. Clarence Mackay invited me to a concert in his beautiful house after dinner, where I met some of the American men that I am most devoted to—Mr. Polk, our ex-Ambassador Mr. Davis, and Colonel House. I sat next to the latter with whom I had a good talk and, what with hearing Kreisler—the greatest living violinist—and being in a position to observe the glowing enthusiasm of Elizabeth and the melancholy expression of her husband, I was consoled for the midnight journey which we took to Washington when the party was over.

My love for my grand-baby, the titter of talk, the tissue paper of unpacking outside my door, and the miawling of "Minnie" the cat, prevented me from resting upon my arrival in the morning, and when I went to the Senate after lunch I could hardly keep awake. The Four Power Treaty was being discussed, but the debate was languid, and more seats were unoccupied than Senators speaking.

Except for a tribune, the Senate reminds me of the *Chambre* in Paris. Everyone walks about, and you cannot be sure that any of the Senators will speak from the seat that they occupied the day before, which makes it rather confusing to a stranger.

At 4.30 I went to see Mr. Hughes in the Department of State. He is remarkably handsome and has not only a striking intelligence, but charming manners. We said nothing worth recording. I told him what, alas! he must have heard a thousand times: the profound impression that his opening speech on Disarmament at the

Washington Conference had created in my country, if not all over the world; and what perhaps he did not know so well, that there never was a closer feeling than that which exists between England and America to-day.

When I say this with all the eloquence I can command at every lecture, though it is always cheered, it is seldom reported, and I read in one of the papers:

"What Mrs. Margot Asquith said about the hand-clasp of Great Britain and the United States is doubtful if not conventional," I am glad to be called conventional, but what I say is not doubtful; it is true.

I see that in one of Byron's recently published letters, he writes to Lady Melbourne:

"I wish that ... would not speak his speech at the Durham meeting above once a week after its first delivery.

"Ever yours most nepotically,

"B."

But in spite of Byron's wise warning I repeat the same thing in every lecture, because I feel passionately that it is not only important that the English-speaking nations should stand side by side, but vital to the Peace of Europe, and I am far from original in thinking it.

XI.
SYRACUSE AND BUFFALO

CITY OF CULTURE AND BEAUTY—NIAGARA'S NATURAL
BEAUTY MARRED BY BILLBOARDS—MARGOT READS ABOUT
HERSELF

ON March 13 my daughter and her husband motored me to
Baltimore where, after speaking to a responsive audience, we took
the midnight train to Utica, and went from there to the Onondaga
Hotel at Syracuse. This is a university city of culture and beauty, and
I wished I had had time to see more of it.

I was introduced to my audience by Dean Richards, a lady of ability
and high standing in the college, and several people came up and
spoke to me behind the scenes when the lecture was over.

I have received many remarkable letters and invitations in every city
I have visited, not only to lunch and dine, but even to stay in private
houses. Had I but realised the great distances over here when I left
England, I would have started earlier, and made a longer tour, but I
am going home for my son's Easter holidays and have therefore been
obliged to refuse much hospitality. In case anyone reads these
impressions, I would like them to know how deeply their
spontaneous generosity has touched me. I will quote a letter which
was put into my hands at Syracuse:

March 13, 1922.

"*Mrs. Asquith*,
"DEAR MADAM,

"When a person has bestowed upon another a gift—such as 'The
Diary of Margot Asquith'—ought not the favoured one to give an
expression of appreciation to the donor? I think so. And this
conviction must be the excuse for my making so bold as to address
you, Mrs. Asquith, to thank you for giving us—who live in so
different a world to that of yours—a glimpse of your spirit, so
colorful, so vivid, so noble. And the charm of it is that this color,
vividness, verve, and charm is not carried consciously and heavily—
but is borne lightly, charmingly, like an ornament,—a jewel.

"I am not young, nor given to raptures; I am older than you, and I
am only thanking you for the radiance your writings have thrown

upon my life; and when to-morrow night I see and hear you at the Opera House in Syracuse, you may perhaps care to know that one among many happy people is enjoying a completeness she had not dreamed would come to her.

"With all good wishes to Mrs. Asquith here on our shores, and beyond the sea, I am,

"Sincerely yours,

"E. A. S——."

There have been other letters I would like to quote, but for fear of boring my readers I will end with the following, written from Chicago,

"To Margot Asquith,

"I read your volume a year ago and at once decided if it was a girl I would call her 'Margot.'

"Tuesday night at Orchestra Hall I heard and saw you. Your enthusiasm, your zest for life, the airy grace of your movements, and the charm of your smile will live in my memory always.

"Here's hoping that some of the wealth of your qualities will go with the name 'Margot' to my little one.

"May you live long, Margot Asquith, is the wish of,

"M. M. F.——."

On the 16th we arrived at Buffalo, where, after seeing the usual army of photographers and reporters, we motored twenty-five miles out to Niagara.

I had always imagined the drive to the Falls would have been long, slow, dangerous, and steep; that this amazing spectacle must be situated in a wild and lonely place, with possibly one romantic hotel encircled by balconies for the convenience of tourists who had travelled from great distances to see it; whereas it is approached by a straight, flat, and crowded road, with tram-cars pursuing their steady course the whole way from Buffalo City. The Niagara Falls, so far from being in a lonely spot, are surrounded by gasometers, steel factories, and chimney pots. Of their beauty and magnificence it would be as ridiculous as it would be presumptuous for me to write, but when my maid said she had expected them to be more "outlandish," I did not contradict her.

Mr. Horton's brother told me of an Irishman who, on being asked to express his opinion, answered, "I don't see what is to prevent the water from going over," but I felt almost too depressed to laugh.

You might have supposed that the whole neighbouring population would have risen like an army to protest against a hideous city of smoke and steel being erected round the glorious Falls of Niagara, and it was characteristic of the population of Buffalo that our chauffeur did not pull up at the Falls, but, upon our stopping him, said he had presumed we wanted to go to the power station.

If I ever return to America, I should not be surprised if a line of safe-sailing steamships had been engineered to go down the Niagara Falls.

I do not think that in Scotland either the country of Scott or the Ettrick shepherd, nor the passes of Killiecrankie or Glencoe, will ever be deformed for commercial purposes.

As a complete outsider with a short and hurried experience of the United States, this has struck me more than anything else. Beauty, which is so obvious in the architecture and other things, seems to be underestimated, and where nature should dominate, I have been shocked on every road that I have travelled by the huge billboards and advertisements of the most flamboyant kind, which irritate the eye and distort the vision of what otherwise would be unforgettable and inspiring. It is much the same everywhere. In Chicago the Michigan Boulevard, with the lovely lake on one side and grand buildings on the other, running at enormous width for a long distance, is one of the finest broadways in the world; but it is spoilt by a vulgar erection at the end, advertising something or other against the sky, in electric bulbs of rapid and changing colours.

I found the people I met were chiefly interested in the following report of indignation meetings:

"Blame Girls for 'Snugglepupping' and 'Petting Parties' in Chicago."

"Male 'Flappers' Parents hold Indignation Meeting."

"Boys who don't follow Fair Companions' Pace called 'Sissies, Poor Boobs and Flat Tires'."

I have only seen two headings that have really interested me. One was:

"A Good Name."

The other: "Wanted, a Rare Man: aggressive yet industrious, fighting, yet tactful and dignified. He must have a good education, and an appearance which will give him an entrée into the best homes."

I would much like to be presented to any of the men who will answer these advertisements, though I have no doubt they are tumbling over one another.

From Buffalo we went on to Cincinnati where I read in one of the newspapers:

"MARGOT

"Margot Asquith, wife of the former Prime Minister of England, is in Cincinnati.

"Men who like to believe that they know more than their wives would not be happy with a woman like Margot for wife. She knows more than most men, and there is scarcely anything she cannot or will not talk about.

"She wrote a book that is an encyclopedia of the inside history of British politics and history of her time.

"There aren't many like Margot. Husbands who long after the honeymoon like to be entertained will envy Asquith his Margot. It must be pleasant to have a Margot in the house."

I expect the writer was pulling my leg—to use a slang expression— or possibly pitying my husband, but it amused me.

XII.
INTERESTING ST. LOUIS

MET BY THE MAYOR—ANOTHER INTELLIGENT REPORTER—
NEWS FROM HOME AND VIEWS THEREON—LUNCHEON AT
WOMEN'S CLUB

WE were met at St. Louis station by a vast crowd of photographers, reporters—male and female—headed by the Mayor, a grand fellow called Henry W. Kiel. He motored me to the Hotel Statler where my rooms were full of roses and, in spite of an iron bed, we were more than comfortable. I am like stuff that is guaranteed not to wash, so I sat down at once to talk to the reporters, among whom I observed one man of supreme intelligence. Caustic and bitter, he interrupted the females and asked to be allowed to return to us after dinner. Mr. Paul Anderson and I had a first rate discussion, while my secretary typed and telephoned till, with his usual consideration, he came back to send me to bed, where I remained like a trout on a bank with piles of old *Times's* which Mr. Anderson had brought me.

I read details, for the first time, of Mr. Montague's resignation, and smiled over the belated theory of the joint responsibility of our British Cabinet. When one recalls the many conflicting opinions expressed by every minister without rebuke, culminating in the Admiralty note upon the Geddes Report, the Prime Minister's indignation is more than droll. I presume the Conservative wing of the Coalition wanted to get rid of Indian Reform as interpreted by the Viceroy and Mr. Montague, and I shall watch with interest the action that Lord Reading will take upon the matter.

Arresting Ghandi was as unwise as stealing a cow from a temple; but from such a distance political comment may be as belated as the theory of cabinet responsibility; and the inspired agitator—beloved of his people—may, for all I know, be governing India at the present moment.

St. Louis is among the most interesting cities I have visited. The Mississippi is commanded upon both its banks by huge buildings, and spanned by grand bridges. There is a private park as large as the Bois de Boulogne, and an open air theatre with oak trees on either side of the stage. The school buildings and Washington College are of perfect architecture, and I was grateful to Mrs. Moore—a woman of sympathy and authority—for driving me out to a lovely club house for tea, which gave me an opportunity of seeing the environment.

I was entertained the next day at a private luncheon given by a ladies' club and was glad to be sitting next to dear Mrs. Moore. Observing a single gentleman seated among the company I asked in a whisper who he was; upon being told he was a reporter I said, in an aside to my other neighbour, that for the rest of the meal I would confine my remarks to: "Yes," "No," or "I wonder!" and "How true!" Upon this the unfortunate young man was conducted from the room. He had a peculiarly charming face and when I saw what had happened I said I was afraid I also would have to leave the table, as I could not allow any guest to be insulted for my sake; at which he was allowed to return. I apologised to him, saying that though I had imagined this to be an informal gathering at which no newspapers would be represented, I did not wish him to be treated with any lack of courtesy, and hoped he would not make copy out of any foolish thing I might have said. He was particularly nice and, although I shall probably never see what he has written about me, I am willing to "take a chance"—as they express it over here.

After signing my name twenty-three times—as flattering as it was fatiguing—the Mayor came to fetch me away. Mrs. Moore and two other ladies accompanied us on a motor drive to see the city. The Mayor—who is a big man—sat rather uncomfortably between me and Mrs. Moore, and said that, with the permission of the other two ladies he proposed to put his arm round my waist as, being engaged to speak at a meeting of the Boy Scouts, he would be unable to attend my lecture in the evening. I told him that, after this, nothing but bribery and corruption could re-elect him as the Mayor of St. Louis.

"Then I shall return to my original occupation, Mrs. Asquith; I started life as a bricklayer, and I have not forgotten my trade, at which I am unrivalled."

The ladies said he was much more likely to be returned as their political representative, and after asking "Joe," his chauffeur, to stop and enable him to buy me cigarettes, he took me back to the hotel.

I found a beautiful bouquet of orchids on my table to which was pinned a card from one of the ladies whom I had met at lunch:

"From Mrs. Hocker, with best wishes for a successful evening at St. Louis, to absolutely the most brilliant and interesting woman it has been my privilege to meet either in America or Europe."

I need hardly say that I clung to my bouquet that evening when I was escorted upon the stage by Judge Henry Caulfield, the City Counsellor.

Mr. Anderson of the St. Louis *Post-Dispatch* returned to talk to us after the meeting, and I can truly say that after "Bruce" — whose real name I never discovered — I found him the most interesting press-man that I have met. I wrote to his editor congratulating him on having such a man upon his staff, and received a grateful reply.

Never having been interviewed till I arrived in this country, I do not know in what way reporters of intellect here would compare with ours, but it passes my comprehension to understand why those that I have met are content to write for papers that seldom print what is either informing or interesting.

One of them said to me:

"We do not publish news, Mrs. Asquith, we concoct it."

XIII.
KANSAS CITY AND OMAHA

AMERICAN VOICES RARELY MUSICAL—SEES LOVELY
COUNTRY HOME—DISCUSSION ON CHARACTER BUILDING—
MARGOT PREDICTS GREAT FUTURE FOR GOVERNOR ALLEN

WE travelled to Kansas City the night of the lecture and were met upon our arrival and taken to the country house of Mrs. Edwin Shields.

After greeting her, I observed her fine tapestries, oriental china, portraits (by Sir Joshua Reynolds), and other old masters, as well as modern French pictures. We ate porridge, eggs and bacon and grapefruit for breakfast, off an oak table with Irish linen napkins, and I observed the refinement of my hostess's little face, and the pretty quality of her voice.

I do not think the voices here are generally musical; they are nasal and a little loud and, though Americans have a great deal of geniality and love of fun, I am so slow at picking up the language, that I probably miss much of the irony and *finesse* that characterises our better kind of humour. The Canadians, who are of British stock, have a better sense of humour; but it is always a dangerous subject to write about, and when I remember the stupid things that evoke the laughter of the London public in our theatres, I feel I had better walk warily.

I am Scotch, and as a nation we have been accused of lack of humour; I cannot be expected to agree with this, nevertheless I remember being told in my youth of a man who had said:

"Oh! aye; Jock undoubtedly jokes, but he jokes with facility. I joke too, but with difficulty."

The French have a far finer sense of humour than any other nation in the world, and all they say is a constant source of delight to me.

It is pardonable not to laugh at what is amusing, but sudden guffaws at bad jokes is the test of a true sense of humour.

After breakfasting with Mrs. Shields I asked her to show me over her beautiful house. I was reminded of Glen by the freshness of the chintzes, and general feeling of air and comfort which I saw wherever I went.

We started at midday for Omaha, where we arrived in the evening. I felt less sad at parting with my hostess as I knew I was going to spend from 7 a.m. till midnight with her on the 24th. She is coming to Europe this summer where I shall look forward to entertaining her in London, as well as in the country.

After leaving her, Mr. Horton told me she had said to him that till she met me, she felt like a flower that had grown on clay soil, and that I had helped her to break into the sunlight. I was deeply touched, and am encouraged to hope that some day I may be worthy of so rare a compliment.

Upon our arrival at Omaha we were met by an open motor lent by Mrs. Kountze, who had invited us to stay with her in her town house, but fearing that three of us might be embarrassing, we decided to go to the hotel.

Omaha is a lovely city, with avenues of trees on either side of wide boulevards, and within easy reach of stretches of wild and beautiful country. As our hostess had been obliged to go to New York, her kind relations conducted us to see the wonderful views surrounding the town.

After speaking in the afternoon to an encouraging audience, with Mr. Hall, the British Consul, as my chairman, I dined with Mr. and Mrs. Ward Burgess. They were more than hospitable, and had it not been for the severe figure of my secretary standing in the doorway, my jolly host, who had entertained me for two hours at dinner, would have prevented me from catching the midnight train.

We returned to Kansas City early on the morning of the 24th.

On being informed by Mrs. Shields's butler that her maid had already called her, I had a bath and, dressing as quickly as I could, went downstairs.

Her sitting room was a garden of roses, lilies and antirrhinums and I shall always remember our unforgettable *tête-à-tête*.

We started upon personality, and the difficulty of expressing what was true without hurting anyone, or acquiring character without becoming a character part. The difference between originality and eccentricity; kindness and tenderness; sympathy and understanding; and the delicate grades by which your attempts at goodness may either help or hamper your fellow creatures.

It is an eternal problem; and the morally lenient and socially severe is what you encounter every day of your life. I confessed how much I resented the shortness of life and urged her to realise this, as she appeared to me, in spite of having a genius for friendship, to be self-contained and lonely. She was responsive, and said many encouraging things to me. I said that somewhere or other I had read that Marcus Aurelius had begged us to keep our colour. I was not very sure of the correct text; but that the idea was that some of us were born red, some yellow, and others grey, but that however this might be, the point was to keep it; not so much by contrast or conflict with the other person, but to complement it. Great scientists, mathematicians or philosophers may manage to develop their personality alone, but what they write will not have the key that the writings of men who are nearer the earth are able to present to ordinary human beings.

At one of Abraham Lincoln's great meetings, he had to walk through the crowd to reach the platform. He heard someone say as he passed:

"Is *that* President Lincoln? Why, what a common-looking fellow!"

At which he turned round and said:

"God likes common-looking fellows or he would not have made so many of them."

I told her how much I had been moved by her remark to my secretary that our friendship would help her to emerge out of clay soil; adding that the desire of my life was to replant myself in a bigger pot every year, and that what she had said would encourage me to go on. After a certain age we were liable to become stationary; and the ravages of war so far from having regenerated, had retarded civilisation.

We were interrupted by Mr. Henry J. Allen, a guest who arrived long before the luncheon hour.

The Governor of the State of Kansas is a man of authority—not only intelligent but intellectual, always a rare combination, and it needs no witch to predict a great future for him. He remained at Mrs. Shields's lovely house in Cherry Street from 11.30 till 6 in the evening, in spite of having an appointment at 4, by which I inferred he could do what he liked.

XIV.
THE WAR AND PROHIBITION

HEATED DISCUSSION ON ENGLAND'S ENTRY INTO THE WAR—OUR GERMAN FRIENDS—AMERICAN VITALITY—MISQUOTED ON PROHIBITION

I sat next to Mr. Heath Moore at lunch and discussed many subjects; among others, the motives that had brought Great Britain into the war. He expressed himself with vigour and frankness, and said that nothing would induce him to believe that our purpose had been moral. That our trade was in danger of being out-rivalled, and the German navy had developed into such a formidable menace, that after France had been defeated, our own shores would have been immediately attacked by the Germans; it was therefore humbug to suggest that our motive had not been one of pure self defence.

As this was the first anti-British note that I had heard since my arrival, it interested me.

I asked him where he imagined our ships would be when the German dreadnoughts sailed into our harbours: and what sort of reception the British people were likely to give the enemy crew, even supposing it could land an army—never a very easy matter—and concluded by saying I had not been kept awake by the fear that the Kaiser would succeed where Napoleon had failed. He stuck to his point and said that but for the violation of Belgium we would not have entered into the war. I answered that no doubt this had made it easier for the party in power—of which my husband was the head—because among the many convictions that divide Liberals from Conservatives is that we believe in freedom, while they believe in force: and that imperialism meant militarism against which we would fight for ever. But, I added, no British Government of whatever party would have watched with folded arms the whole German navy sail down our coast to attack France.

He inquired if my husband had felt any qualms *when he took upon his shoulders this great decision.* I answered that our Foreign Secretary, Sir Edward now Lord Grey, Lord Crewe, and others, had made up their minds from the first moment; and that in one year—thanks to the Committee of Defence, Lord Haldane and Lord Kitchener—we had produced a large voluntary army; and had he been in England at the time, he would have been struck by the pathos and silence with which men of every class joined up to fight in a war which was not their own, against a foe for whom they felt no hatred.

He asked if England had been disappointed that America had come in so late to help her, I confessed that in a moment of pique I had exclaimed that had I been Christopher Columbus I would have said nothing about the discovery, but that I doubted if Great Britain would have come in any earlier to help the United States had they been in a similar quandary.

Someone asked me privately if I had lost a child in the war. I said that my little boy had been too young to fight, but that both my sisters, my three brothers and my husband had lost their sons; that living in Downing Street in the first years of the war had been an anguish, the depth of which no one could realise.

We had refused to drop any of our German friends in London, and in consequence became targets for the abuse and calumny of our social and political enemies.

It is a subject that rouses me to undying indignation when I remember the manner in which we were persecuted, not only by our opponents, but by some of my personal friends even after we had been defeated in the General Election of 1918. One of the candidates said that she had often been to Downing Street on matters of vital importance during the war and had been struck by the lack of feeling shown by myself and my husband.

Mr. Heath Moore gave me an account of the savage manner with which the German population over here had been treated when America joined the Allies. He told me among other things, that one of his fellow-countrymen in a great recruiting speech had been interrupted by a man in the gallery who was understood to have shouted: "Hurrah for the Kaiser!" At which he was kicked and beaten down the stairs to the street and, but for the intervention of a policeman, would have been killed. When asked what he had done, the unfortunate German said his only son had been killed in the war and that he had shouted: "To hell with the Kaiser!"

This was mild compared to some of the cruelties related.

It is always dangerous to generalise, but the American people, while infinitely generous, are a hard and strong race and, but for the few cemeteries I have seen, I am inclined to think they never die. They thrive in rooms as hot as conservatories, can sit up all night, eat candy and ice-cream all day, and live to a great age upon either social or commercial excitement without leisure.

When I left the room to rest and think over my lecture, I was afraid I had not shown sufficient consideration to Mr. Heath Moore or his opinions, so that I was relieved on being informed that he had proposed himself to return to dinner the same evening. I hope we shall meet each other again, as he is a man of compassion.

I lectured after dinner, and before I had finished I fixed my eyes upon Mr. Heath Moore sitting next to Mrs. Shields and spoke of the moral motives that had made Great Britain enter into the war, apart from her friendship with France. I said that while the French had sacrificed everything and fought magnificently, other countries had been animated by the same motives, and in the end it had been won by a League of Nations.

I dwelt at length upon the cruelty with which the Germans had been treated in the United States and at home, and was cheered when I said that had Christ come down among the civilian population at any time during the war His sense of justice and compassion would have earned for Him the title of pro-German.

We went back to Cherry Street before taking the midnight train.

I was introduced to several people of the City of Kansas at supper, all of whom I found interesting. One man said to me:

"I knew you had charm and personality, Mrs. Asquith, but you must have spoken on a hundred platforms to have acquired such courage and eloquence."

I gazed at him dumb with surprise.

When I left I promised to write to my hostess and Mr. Moore.

* * * * * * *

We changed at St. Louis, on our way to Indianapolis, and were met there at 7 a.m. the next morning by Mr. Paul Anderson; we all had breakfast at the station together, and I was sorry to say good-bye to him.

I read quoted from a London paper that Mr. Balfour—the greatest living Commoner—had been made a Knight of the Garter.

We were met upon our arrival in the afternoon at Indianapolis by Mr. and Mrs. Sullivan, and accompanied to their house by a reporter, I was surprised to see in the papers next day that I had said among other things that in Scotland we were not only highly educated, but able to study in our schools both the French and Spanish languages, and were I the Queen of America I would restore drink.

I began to fear that, though uncrowned, I must have in a fit of absence usurped some of the powers I had indicated ought to be restored to the United States.

After travelling all day on the 26th, we arrived in sousing rain at night to hear there were no porters at the station. On enquiring if they were on strike, I was told that there never had been any porters at Kalamazoo.

Loaded with luggage, we paddled like ducks in the mud to an inferior hotel.

As we had lunched at midday and there was no dining car on the train, we were annoyed to hear that no one could get any food after 8.30 p.m., but luckily for us there were still ten minutes before the restaurant closed, so we devoured what we could. On the next day I was told by reporters and other people that an eminent divine had said in a sermon that, thanks to my belief in intemperance, I was not a fit and proper person to give a lecture, and in consequence, my audience of the evening was not all that I could have desired. I had something to say about bearing false witness against your neighbour, but the few that were there were more than enthusiastic, and I was embraced by a woman from Peebleshire.

I was grateful to have the following cutting posted to me:

"Can't stand the Tone of a Morning Contemporary in Reporting Mrs. Asquith's Address,

"Editor, Evening Telegram:

"Sir,—I am a busy man, and have not much time to write letters, but I can't stand the sneering, cheap remarks of the *Globe* in their account of Mrs. Asquith's summing up of 'prohibition.'

"Mrs. Asquith did not give stories of a 'vulgar nature,' 'depicting an individual half-stupid with drink.' Note the hard Pharisaical way in which they gloat over the word 'drink.' Reminds me of the cheap old-fashioned 'temperance' poems. Mrs. Asquith quite properly and honestly called attention to the farce of prohibition laws, and merely voiced the opinion of ninety per cent of all honest people when she decried the unjust and unconstitutional 'blue laws' which the bigoted and ignorant minority of the Canadian and American people are trying to enact and enforce on the unwilling majorities—the real taxpayers.

"Would to goodness we had more such women, fearlessly candid, broadminded, and un-hypocritical like the same Margot Asquith. England, with all her faults, will never pander to the few fanatics who are the real oppressors, depressors and joy-killers.

"F. J. Paget."

XII.
NEW YORK IDEAL CITY

LIFE AND AIR AND GAIETY IN NEW YORK—LETTER FROM GOVERNOR ALLEN—MARGOT MEETS ARTHUR BRISBANE—PRINCESS BIBESCO'S BOOK

AFTER travelling two days and a night we arrived in New York on the evening of the 28th to find Elizabeth and her husband waiting for the elevator to take them to a play; they were ready to throw this over but I told them I was too exhausted to talk and only longed to get to bed.

I have not been to San Francisco, but if I were an American I would live in New York City. St. Louis, Syracuse, Omaha, Washington, are more beautiful because of their environment; but there is life in the air, and a general atmosphere of gaiety and movement which I find infinitely stimulating in New York.

We saw "The Truth about Blayds" and "Kiki," two plays that were wonderfully acted; I enjoyed every moment of "Blayds," and the heroine of "Kiki" would make her fortune in any play.

On Sunday the 2nd of April I went to tea at the studio of my friend Mrs. Komroff. I have known her for many years, when she was Nellie Barnard, and I do not believe there is any artist living who can paint children in water-colour in the manner she does. The room was crowded with friends and artists and the portraits that were displayed filled us with admiration.

Together with many letters from home I received the following from Governor Allen.

"STATE OF KANSAS
"OFFICE OF THE GOVERNOR
"TOPEKA

"THE GOVERNOR.   "March 30, 1922

"MY DEAR MRS. ASQUITH,

"I am taking the liberty of sending you a copy of my book on the industrial question. I hope you will forgive me for intruding it upon you. I have so many delightful recollections of the keen and instructive things you said at Mrs. Shields's house that I now find

59

myself full of regret that the conversation continually drifted into general discussions which robbed us all of an opportunity to hear more of your own conclusions.

"Your generous comment upon Kansas City and the west has made us all happy and as a citizen I want to express my hearty appreciation of your compliments to this growing section of the country.

"I do not wonder that you drew from my remarks the conclusion that I am 'illiberal.' I was stupid not to realise that your definition of the word liberal is different from that which characterises it out here just now. In your world, 'liberal' is an honourable word. Over here it has come through misuse to denote a peculiar class whose reaction is antigovernment. The anarchist, the socialist, the communist and the bolshevist are all put down in one class, and the word liberal is thundered at them by orators and editors. It isn't fair to the word.

"If you have time, I'd be awfully glad if you would look over 'The Party of the Third Part,' because it relates to a program of industrial peace and justice which the President has recently indorsed in a message to Congress and which New York is now trying to write into her state legislation. Doubtless if the law is held to be constitutional by the Supreme Court of the United States several States in the forthcoming legislative sessions will adopt the principle of impartial adjudication of labor quarrels when those quarrels occur in the essential industries of food, fuel, clothing and transportation.

"I am sincerely glad you came to the middle west and I am grateful to Mrs. Shields for the delightful privilege of meeting you. I hope you will have a safe and happy voyage and that some day you will come back to America.

"Yours sincerely,

"HENRY J. ALLEN."

I was proud and pleased to sit to Baron Meyer one morning, the greatest photographer that ever lived—poor praise for an artist who can express himself in whatever he touches. If I die on the *Mauretania* going home,—which is more than likely as the sea seldom forgives bad sailors—I am certain of leaving something to my family that they can look at without repugnance.

On the 3rd of April we read in the papers "Balfour accepts Peerage: will enter Lords as Earl."

We were entertained at lunch by Mr. Arthur Brisbane, a famous journalist and friend of Elizabeth's. I sat between him and Mr. Hapgood and had an excellent conversation. They both spoke in high praise of "I Have Only Myself to Blame." In connection with this I will quote an American review out of the *New Republic*.

MODERN LOVE

"'I Have Only Myself to Blame,' by Elizabeth Bibesco.

"This book is a collection of pictorial sketches and stories. Its field is restricted. It isn't about life in general. It leaves out religion and science, and illness and wars, animals and politics, and business, and children, and crime. It's only about lovers and loving.

"It is an unsettling book. Just as you have privately made up your mind, perhaps, to be sensible, and be satisfied with what you have— or haven't—and to forget about a oneness with somebody, and are feeling rich enough with much less, this book tells you a story which reaches into some inner part of you that was getting dried up, and makes you feel painfully aware of the things you are missing.

"Here for instance is part of a letter that one woman writes:

"'In a way I don't see why you should ever want to kiss me again. Do you understand what I mean, that I feel so merged, so eternally in your arms that I can hardly believe in the process of being taken into them again and again? Oh my dear, do you notice how one never can use superlatives when they really would mean something? They seem to slink away ashamed of their loose lives. After all we can't "make love" to one another. We both do it too well. This is not an incident, a game, an art; ours is not a love affair, it is life.'

"Another extract: 'I can't sleep. There is something oppressive in the atmosphere.... There is always a tenseness when you are not there, a cumulative unreality. I have felt it all day.... I seemed to be a ghost wandering about in some meaningless void. It was not only that I couldn't believe in the people, I could not even believe in the chairs and tables; it was tiring. You know how in fairy tales the lovely Princess is turned into a toad and has to wait for a kiss to release her, that was what I felt like—that nothing but your touch could make me into a human being again.'

"Her trueness is so exquisite, it really doesn't need any plots. For example, she is describing a man who has fallen in love, and who, though he used to be talkative, can now only stammer. He wants to propose to a beautiful girl but he can't. 'One day they were walking through a bluebell wood.... "I must speak," he said to himself unhappily, while he realised he was physically incapable of bringing out the most common-place phrase....'

"He decided to speak when he saw the next orchis.

"He thought of a woman he had once imagined himself in love with. She had had red hair and green eyes ... and red hair had seemed infinitely wicked and alluring and adventurous....

"He saw an orchis and hastily averted his eyes.

"He thought of a rocking horse he had had as a child, dappled grey with a grey yellow tail and a scarlet saddle....

"Another orchis. He looked at her imploringly.

"'What are you thinking about?' she responded to his appeal.

"'Rocking horses,' he said. 'Will you marry me?' And then desperately, 'I know that's not the way to put it'; and then convulsively, 'I love you.'

"She waited till he had finished and then she said.... 'That's a very nice way to put it.'"

"This seems to one reader at least one of the best proposals in fiction.

"Perhaps these stories are not classics. But they are of the very best of to-day's. They are not only charming, and fresh, but they have a nobility; they are seriously concerned with our lonely emotional needs.

"And there are things in them that touch the very core of one's heart. Things a reader is startled to find in print—things he had supposed not expressible. Secret things that make him whisper, 'Why I thought no one knew that but myself.'

Clarence Day, Jr."

In answer to a letter of thanks from Elizabeth he wrote:
"It made me so sad to read some of the reviews of your book. I knew of course how few people appreciated fine writing, but now I know how few people have ever been in love."

Mr. Heath Moore put this review into my hands before we parted and I thought it was clever of him to know the pleasure it would give me.

XVI.
CRITICISM AND FAREWELL

DOLL SALESMAN TALKS ON PROHIBITION—PERILS OF COMMERCIALISM AND MATERIALISM IN AMERICA—PLEA FOR LOVE AND FRIENDSHIP

ON April 3—the day before I sailed for England—I went out early to buy toys to entertain my grand-baby on our voyage in the *Mauretania*; and had an interesting talk with one of the many civil salesmen that I have met all over the United States in their beautiful shops. He said he regretted that he would not be able to attend my last lecture although he had been to the other three in New York, because he feared the daughter of a friend of his was dying. She was a little girl living in a suburb who had fainted some weeks before. Her mother had given her the only stimulant they had in the house; since when she had suffered from blood-poisoning and was lying in a critical condition.

"I do hope, madam, you will deal to-night with the abominable law of Prohibition. It has encouraged this country to manufacture liquors of the most dangerous kind," he said.

I told him I heard the same complaint wherever I had been and, while sympathising deeply with him, feared I could do no more, as I had dealt freely and at length with the subject.

I was advertised by the following card to make my last speech.

FAREWELL LECTURE
under the auspices of
THE SOCIETY OF FRIENDS OF
ROUMANIA
Founded under the August Patronage of
Her Majesty Queen Marie of Roumania
MARGOT ASQUITH
will close her brilliant and successful tour by
delivering a lecture entitled
IMPRESSIONS OF THE UNITED STATES AND CANADA

I put on my best dress and, armed with a bouquet of rare orchids given to me by my chairman, made my final public appearance in this country.

As Mr. Nelson Cromwell, who introduced me, is a fluent orator and had a great deal to say while paying a fine tribute to my husband — and knowing that I was to hold a reception afterwards — I cut my lecture as short as I could.

Among other subjects, I dealt with the exaggerated belief over here in commercial success; and the dangerous self-interest and lack of leisure which was encouraging not only this but every nation to materialism.

I had read in the morning papers a typical example of what I meant.

"First have what people want.

"Then let them know it.

"*Thorough advertising* is the Secret of Success.

"The old way was to let the people find it out gradually and slowly, in time for your grandson to get rich. The modern way is to have it TO-DAY, and make everybody know it TO-MORROW, or, if possible, THIS AFTERNOON."

I told them what I had observed at the Niagara Falls, and spoke of the many hideous bill boards and advertisements that desecrated the scenery wherever I had been, and pausing over the one among others that had really interested me, "A GOOD NAME", was interrupted by my chairman who exclaimed in a clear voice:

"ASQUITH!"

This met with immense success.

I ended by saying that few countries really cared for one another. It was not rivalry or jealousy that produced this indifference, but a certain blindness of heart. That we were part of the same family, if we would only realise it, and had had a terrible object lesson in imagining that any of us, however much we prepared or tried, could succeed in crushing the other. We had seen enough hate, and enough death; and that I passionately hoped the English-speaking nations all the world over would try a new departure, and do what they could to promote friendship and love.
The next day we sailed for England in the *Mauretania*.

If I were to finish without criticism, it might be said that these pages should not have been called "Impressions," but "Experiences"; and against this I have not only been warned, but adjured.

Nevertheless it is difficult, without appearing unfriendly, to write with candour upon matters that have moved me in my American tour.

It must be said that the architecture, regulations of street-traffic, arrangement of flower-shops, plumbing, and telephone service are infinitely superior to our own, but these are not criticisms, they are facts, the truth of which is not disputed.

I realise that there is not a nation in the world that extends such a generous welcome to the many strangers that go there as the United States. But admiration for my husband, and the publication of the first volume of my autobiography—which aroused both favourable and unfavourable comment—prevented me at the outset from being a complete stranger. Indeed many of the people who attended my lectures seemed to know all about me; and I was surprised when crowding on to the stage they sometimes exclaimed:

"But you are so different to what we expected you would be! And you haven't told us what you think of us."

I begged them to be frank, and tell me without fear of offence what they had imagined I would be like; but they could only repeat:

"I don't know! But somehow we thought you would be the very opposite of what you are."

When I tried a little clumsy chaff by saying: "I am sorry to have disappointed you!" it was always met with a protest; and on one occasion I heard a man say to the woman who was with him:

"There you are! I told you all along; but you wouldn't read the book!" at which the woman grasped me by the hand and said:

"You are writing another volume of your life aren't you, Mrs. Asquith, in which you will tell us everything you think about us."

I explained that I was writing an article on my Impressions of America for immediate publication and the second and final volume of my life which would come out in winter.

Flattering cuttings were sent to me from papers, as: "The Margot myth." And others, which said it was abundantly clear that I was in a chastened humour and, by guarding myself from my critics, was exercising a caution that deprived me of all spontaneity; or words to this effect.

These remarks are of little interest, but they tend to show how much some people and nations depend on the approbation of others and are the reason why I am going to finish with a short summing-up.

XVII.
THINKING IT OVER IN ENGLAND

AMERICANS FRIENDLY BUT VAIN—THE LAND OF THE REFORMER—INTEREST IN EUROPE'S ARISTOCRACY— NEWSPAPERS PANDER TO VULGAR CURIOSITY—PLEA FOR ANGLO-AMERICAN FRIENDSHIP

IT is probably wiser in writing impressions to keep the conclusions you arrive at secret; and many may ask—and with justice—:

"What can a woman know who arrived on the 30th of January, and left on the 4th of April, of America or her people?" In answer to this I can only say that in those nine weeks I saw and talked to more varied types of persons than I could have done had I remained in either New York, Chicago or Washington for as many months. I met and conversed with senators and niggers, farmers and reporters, judges and preachers, hotel proprietors, mayors, solicitors, soldiers, shopmen, doctors, men of science and commerce, and a few of the rarer class of both the fashionable and the leisured. During this experience there are certain things I observed that I shall take the risk of writing down.

The Americans, while the most friendly people in the world, are too much concerned about each other; and, though not personally, they are nationally vain. They would rather hear themselves abused than undiscussed; which inclines one to imagine that they are suffering from the uneasiness of the *nouveaux riches*.

What do you think of us? or, how do you compare our men and women and their clothes and customs with your own? was the substance of every question that was put to me.

There are things of surpassing interest in this country, but have any of us heard an English man or woman ask a foreigner what he thought of us? Or, if they were silly enough to do so, who would be interested in the reply?

Some will say that this comes from pride, or insularity; but they would be wrong. We are not obsessed by the desire to interfere with our neighbour that is noticeable all over America.

In spite of true generosity and kindliness, I was aware of an undercurrent of illiberalism and violence which amazed me.

In every city that I have visited there are clubs, both male and female, to forbid or promote some harmless triviality and until these are ridiculed they will prevent the United States from ever becoming what we should call a free country.

Because there is little gallantry and no reserve, people do not necessarily become of one class. We cannot regulate equality, since we are born with different brains, natures, and environment, and so far from being equal, there is such a rigid regard for precedence in America that you are even congratulated after a dinner party because you have been seated "one off Mrs. — —".

While more than severe on anyone who accepts a title, there was no detail too insignificant about our Court or aristocracy that did not excite an almost emotional interest in my audiences. Every day of my tour I received letters begging me to tell them more about the life and habits of our upper classes or anything that I could "about Princess Mary's underwear."

If these letters had been merely the cackle of the feminine goose who likes writing to an advertised person, I would have torn them up, but they were sometimes signed by men, and often expressed the opinions of important local editors.

One night after I was in bed, having had a long talk with an intellectual reporter upon the dearth of great literature in his country, he rang me up to say his paper was annoyed that he had not brought back an accurate description of my hat and dress.

He apologised profusely, but said that that was what the public really cared for: that none of our discussion upon Lincoln, Edgar Allan Poe or William James's fine style, or anything else of interest would be printed in the morning paper. But what I had said to one of the lady reporters, when we were left to ourselves, about Princess Mary's marriage being one of love, would probably be enlarged by headlines into a paragraph. I said I forgave him for waking me up, but was quite unaware that I had even mentioned our royal family.

The next day I read that I had said I was:

"On smoking terms with Queen Mary."

You may say that certain journalism of a similar kind panders to the same curiosity in what is low and vulgar over here, but it is more harmful in the States because the press has more power.

So far from guiding public opinion, the papers in America stimulate all that is worthless and credulous; and you may search in vain to find careful criticism either upon art, music or international affairs.

England has been called a nation of shop-keepers, but I think we spend as much time upon the moors and playing fields as Americans do in elevators and offices.

Perhaps we waste too much time on grass and games; but it has encouraged a certain aloofness and leisure, which produces a quiet mind.

Whether it is from the difficulties of the climate and the overheated rooms, the voices of even the nicest people appeared to me to be loud, and however generously you may have been entertained, you are left with a sense of suffocation, which it would be difficult to explain.

The excuse of being a young country will not continue to cover the rush and noise and lack of privacy that prevail; and the number of small children that I have seen in hotels, shops and restaurants that go to bed at midnight after sucking candy between enormous meals, is not promising for a nation which is always growing up.

The ingrained idea that, because there is no king and they despise titles, the Americans are a free people is pathetically untrue; and you have only to watch the working of the Prohibition law to see the dangers of repressive legislation. There is a perpetual interference with personal liberty over there that would not be tolerated in England for a week.

It is probably due to our passion for understatement and that we have inherited wise and tested regulations that the British are a law abiding race; but I think if the Americans were given a chance they would be the same. I can only say, if they are not, Democracy will prove as great a failure as Czardom.

It is enormously to the credit of the American public that they have never chosen a bad character in their presidents and have produced, in Abraham Lincoln, a man of genius, ability and courage who will live for ever in the hearts and minds of every country in the world. Nor must we forget that he dominated the people in spite of a campaign of calumny by the press only equalled by the one to which my husband was subjected in the latter days of the war.

Men at the head of affairs must be independent of public opinion if they wish to achieve anything and never try to conciliate a press that, in all fairness, it must be said,—with a few exceptions—does not attempt to guide, for more than a transitory moment, anyone to any goal.

The present Government in America from all I heard—some of its heads I had the honour to meet—seems to be an admirable one, and working smoothly in times of exceptional difficulty. President Harding has had the wisdom to get good men round him and is a man of open mind and wide views himself.

With some of the faults I have found during my tour I am told that "The American Credo"[*] (given to me by my friend Mr. Anderson of the St. Louis *Dispatch*) deals with searching fidelity. I daresay when I read it I shall learn where I have been wrong; but in criticising as I have, I am merely fulfilling the promise I made to write my impressions which at best can be but superficial.

[*] By G. J. Nathan and H. L. Mencken.

Among thoughtful people there is a great deal of pro-American propaganda going on in this country, and in conclusion I would like to say that there is so much that is fine and keen in the American race, so much that is disarming and lovable, that if I have written anything exaggerated or erroneous, I should feel of all people the most ungrateful.

I can only plead to be forgiven where I have erred, as I was not only shown unforgettable courtesy and friendship, but I feel it is vital to the peace of the world that our people and those of the United States should understand and care for one another.

THE END

Lightning Source UK Ltd.
Milton Keynes UK
UKHW011043050821
388368UK00001B/149

9 781006 672460